PLYMOUTH IN THE WORDS OF HER FOUNDERS

A
VISITOR'S GUIDE
TO AMERICA'S HOMETOWN

By

Dr. Paul Jehle

Vision Forum
San Antonio, Texas

In association with
PLYMOUTH ROCK FOUNDATION
1120 Long Pond Road, Plymouth, MA 02360

Vision Forum Ministries
4719 Blanco Rd., San Antonio, Texas 78212

www.visionforum.org

ISBN 9780972417341
Cover design by Al Mendenhall

Printed in the United States of America

PREFACE

Unlike his Victorian predecessor, the modern visitor to Plymouth is often hard-pressed to comprehend what the Pilgrims are all about. He has heard of Plymouth Rock, but finds the modest granite boulder in its Grecian sanctuary puzzling. Why are people getting so excited about this? He may then wander about the waterfront, glancing at various monuments and going aboard *Mayflower II*, or perhaps to Pilgrim Hall, before he dismisses his search for the significance of the Pilgrims and just enjoys talking with Plymouth Plantation's role players or has a good meal in a Plymouth restaurant. Sadly, our visitor has seen everything and understood nothing.

How different was the visit of eighty years ago. The average tourist at the Tercentenary in 1920 arrived well-instructed in the history of the Pilgrims and their religious quest in the new world. He had been schooled to emulate the virtues of the *Mayflower* passengers, and he knew their stories by heart: the religious persecution and exile, the momentous voyage, the terrible first winter, the coming of the Indians, the courtship of Myles Standish, and the rest.

His first sight of Plymouth Rock was thrilling because of the mental images of a wintry landing he had made long before his own. He might not make the automatic association between the Pilgrims and Thanksgiving which modern people do, but he had no doubt about their role as the forefathers of the American nation. If he needed to know more, the typical guidebooks of the time were full of details about each of the markers and shrines that helped tell the inspirational tale.

In Dr. Jehle's book, we have a key which unlocks the significance of Plymouth's monuments unnoticed by modern visitors. By combining the actual words of the Pilgrims and their heirs with his exegesis on the symbolism made tangible in stone, he illuminates the importance that the Pilgrim had for our ancestors. By so doing, he restores the Pilgrim Story to a living tradition. He makes it possible to appreciate the role that the memory of the Pilgrims and their holy mission played in American life, and invites us to join in honoring their piety, courage, and perserverance at a time when such virtues are more necessary than ever. It is no small accomplishment.

—James Baker
*Plymouth historian
and author*

FOREWORD

There have been many guidebooks printed about "America's Hometown." They give information on museums, old houses and activities for residents and tourists alike. All are recommended by the author who has an affinity and love for the town of Plymouth.

This guidebook, however, is unique. It attempts to interpret the specific monuments erected in memory of the Pilgrims, Plymouth's founders. After twenty-four years giving walking tours, researching the monuments and the intent of their sculptors as well as the writings of the Pilgrims, I have let the founders of Plymouth interpret the symbols erected in their memory.

Let their words inspire you to restore faith in God, their courage awaken in you the desire to preserve liberty, and their sacrifice strengthen your resolve to train your children to do the same.

—Paul Jehle

DEDICATION

In dedication to:

John and Rosalin Talcott of Plymouth—
founders of Plymouth Rock Foundation who
first introduced me to the Pilgrim Story, and
have sacrificed much to see it preserved for
future generations.

TABLE OF CONTENTS

PART ONE

PART TWO

PART ONE

Plymouth Rock from the Water

THE WATERFRONT MONUMENTS

MAYFLOWER II
THE VOYAGE OF THE PILGRIMS

The Mayflower II under Sail

"… after long beating at sea they fell with that land which is called Cape Cod, the which being made and certainly known to be it, they were not a little joyful." Bradford's description of the *Mayflower*'s arrival at Cape Cod in 1620

9

The Pilgrims left Delftshaven, Holland on July 22, 1620, in the *Speedwell* which they had purchased so they could fish and help pay back the investors who were putting money into their expedition. Only about forty six men, women and children got aboard out of the Pilgrim congregation which had risen to about 300 during their eleven year stay in Leyden. This small vessel was bound for Southhampton,

England, where they would meet up with about seventy-four others aboard the hired *Mayflower* which had sailed from London to meet them.

However, several families would be leaving behind wives and children, and even their pastor, John Robinson, would be staying behind to tend to the majority of the members of the church who could not at this time make such a voyage. Bradford describes this departure from Delftshaven and it is from his comment that the "Separatists" became known as "Pilgrims," (taken from Hebrews 11:13 of the Bible).

EMBARKATION PAINTING

Embarkation Painting from Pilgrim Hall
(used by permission-Pilgrim Society)

"So being ready to depart, they had a day of solemn humiliation... pouring out prayers to the Lord with great fervency, mixed with abundance of tears. And the time being come that they must depart, they were accompanied with most of their brethren out of the city, unto a town sundry miles off called Delftshaven, where the ship lay ready to receive them. So they left that goodly and pleasant city which had been their resting place near twelve years, but they knew they were pilgrims, and looked not much on those things, but lifted up their eyes to the heavens, their dearest country, and quieted their spirits."[48]
Bradford's description of the Embarkation from Holland

After this first emotional separation, they joined with those passengers and crew members who were waiting for them in Southhampton. After facing some hard decisions regarding the contract with their investors (which had changed without their knowing it), the two ships with probably around 120 Pilgrims and adventurists, along with possibly twenty-five total crew members, set sail for the new world on August 5.

A smooth trip across the Atlantic would not be what they would experience, for by August 13, they were turning back to Dartmouth, England to tend to the leaking *Speedwell*. After they had spent some of their precious provisions on repairs, they set sail together again on August 23. However, they turned back again when the *Speedwell* continued to leak, and eventually abandoned her.

With some of their provisions spent, and a great deal of time lost, they made a most difficult decision to part with eighteen of their passengers, sell the *Speedwell* for well below what they paid for it, and continue their voyage with 102 passengers. Bradford describes this second parting with some of their company in the style that has made him famous. Bradford looks for an explanation to events in terms of faith and Biblical analogies.

MAYFLOWER AT HER DOCK IN PLYMOUTH

Mayflower II at her Dock

"And thus, like Gideon's army, this small number was divided, as if the Lord by this work of His providence thought these few too many for the great work He had to do."[49] Bradford describing the parting of eighteen of their number

They finally set sail in the *Mayflower* on September 6, 1620. Bradford records several events that occurred during the voyage.

Seasickness

"These troubles being blown over, and now all being compact together in one ship, they put to sea again with a prosperous wind, which continued divers days together, which was some encouragement unto them; yet, according to the usual manner, many were afflicted with seasickness."[50]

One of the Crew Dies

"And I may not omit here a special work of God's providence. There was a proud and very profane young man, one of the seamen, of a lusty, able body, which made him the more haughty; he would always be condemning the poor people in their sickness and cursing them daily with grievous execrations, and did not hesitate to tell them that he hoped to help to cast half of them overboard before they came to their journey's end, and to make merry with what they had; and if he were by any gently reproved, he would curse and swear most bitterly. But it pleased God before they came half seas over, to smite this young man with a grievous disease, of which he died in a desperate manner, and so was himself the first that was thrown overboard. Thus his

curses light on his own head, and it was an astonishment to all his fellows for they noted it to be the just hand of God upon him."[51]

Mayflower in a storm – painting
(used by permission-Pilgrim Society)

THE MAIN BEAM CRACKS

"After they had enjoyed fair winds and weather for a season, they were encountered many times with cross winds and met with many fierce storms with which the ship was shroudly shaken, and her upper works made very leaky; and one of the main beams in the midships was bowed and cracked, which put them in some fear that the ship could not be able to perform the voyage... But examining all opinions, the master and others affirmed they knew the ship to be strong and firm under water; and for the buckling of the main beam, there was a great iron screw the passengers brought out of Holland, which would raise the beam into his place; the which being done... he would make it sufficient. So

they committed themselves to the will of God and resolved to proceed."[52]

The giant screw could have been a jack to help raise the roofs of their future homes. In any case, it was thought providential that such a screw was on board so that they could complete their journey.

JOHN HOWLAND FALLS OVERBOARD

"In sundry of these storms the winds were so fierce and the seas so high, as they could not bear a knot of sail, but were forced to hull for divers days together. And in one of them, as they thus lay at hull in a mighty storm, a lusty young man called John Howland, coming upon some occasion above the gratings was, with a seele of the ship, thrown in the sea; but it pleased God that he caught hold of the topsail halyards which hung overboard and ran out at length. Yet he held his hold (though he was sundry fathoms under water) till he was hauled up by the same rope to the brim of the water, and then with a boat hook and other means got into the ship and his life saved. And though he was something ill with it, yet he lived many years after and became a profitable member both in church and commonwealth."[53]

After a sixty-six day voyage, they sighted land November 9, on the outer edge of Cape Cod. Attempting to go south to the mouth of the Hudson River where they intended to settle, they were unable to navigate around the dangerous shoals on the outer Cape. Turning back, they anchored in what is now Provincetown harbor, Saturday, November 11.

Before going on shore to explore, knowing they were away from their original destination, and due to the talk of some to leave them and not be under the general agreement, they drew up the Mayflower Compact, a remarkable document of self-government; an extension of their understanding of voluntary and church covenants.

Though not everyone on the ship was a Pilgrim separatist, even the "strangers" (as Bradford called them) signed the document. The original has been lost, and thus we are not sure exactly how many signatures were subscribed. Part of the famous Compact reads as follows:

PROVINCETOWN MAYFLOWER STONE

Signing of the Mayflower Compact
Memorial Stone

"In the Name of God, Amen. We whose names are underwritten, the loyal subjects of our dread Sovereign Lord King James, by the Grace of God of Great Britain, France, and Ireland King, Defender of the Faith... Having undertaken for the glory of God and advancement of the Christian faith and Honor of our King and Country, a Voyage to plant the First Colony in the Northern Parts of Virginia, do by these presents solemnly and mutually in the presence of God and one of another, Covenant and Combine ourselves together into a Civil Body Politic, for our better ordering and preservation and furtherance of the ends aforesaid..."[54]

PROVINCETOWN MAYFLOWER COMPACT MEMORIAL

Mayflower Compact Memorial in Provincetown

Though the Pierce Patent, issued one year later, gave official English permission for the colony, properly designating their new location, there is no doubt that the Mayflower Compact was the seed of their action to form a body of laws as early as 1636 that ordered their commonwealth as a miniature constitution. Such self-government became the cornerstone of American government.

The *Mayflower* returned to England in April of 1621, but not one Pilgrim returned with her! The ship was dismantled in 1624, but what became of the ships beams is not known. Many have wondered why more did not die during the voyage. One of the reasons for this was that the *Mayflower* was a merchant wine ship, and her beams soaked with her cargo. This sanitized the boat and probably kept disease from spreading.

18

For the tercentenary celebration in 1920, a replica ship was made by John Campbell of Boston from the coaster named *Fannie Hall*. On July 6, 1921, on a Wednesday afternoon, the replica ship was towed by a steam tug with a larger than authentic crew and camera men on board. It remained anchored in Plymouth, having come from Provincetown to re-enact the landing of the Pilgrims.

On September 22, 1956, a replica hull, without superstructure or masts, slid into the waters off the shores of Brixham, Devon, England, as the Somerset Light Infantry played *The Battle Hymn of the Republic*. On April 20, 1957, the *Mayflower II* replica sailed from Plymouth England on a recreated voyage. It took a south-westerly route instead of the northern route of the original voyage. About 200 miles off the coast of Bermuda, very heavy weather was experienced and the crew understood what it must have been like to pitch and roll at thirty-eight degrees! The ships of that period were made to *roll* water off the deck, not *keep* water off the deck.

Mayflower II sailed to Nantucket, then Provincetown and into Plymouth, with the voyage lasting fifty-five days, eleven shorter than the original. The crew consisted of thirty two men and on June 13, reached Plymouth. This replica ship has remained in Plymouth for over forty years. Under the direction of Plymouth Plantation it is a favorite tourist spot for millions of people. The ship reminds us continually of the faith and courage of those Separatists, strangers and crew members who crossed the Atlantic for freedom of conscience in 1620.

THE PLYMOUTH ROCK MONUMENT
THE LANDING OF THE PILGRIMS

Plymouth Rock Portico from land

"On Monday they sounded the harbor and found it fit for shipping, and marched into the land and found divers cornfields and little running brooks, a place (as they supposed) fit for situation."[55]
Bradford's description of the Pilgrims landing in Plymouth

After celebrating their first Sabbath within the sight of land on Sunday, November 12, they landed at Provincetown.

LANDING IN PROVINCETOWN

Landing Marker in Provincetown

"Being thus arrived in a good harbor, and brought safe to land, they fell upon their knees and blessed the God of Heaven who had brought them over the vast and furious ocean, and delivered them from all the perils and miseries thereof, again to set their feet on the firm and stable earth, their proper element."[56] Bradford describing the landing at Provincetown

After landing they washed their clothes and began exploring Monday, November 13. The Shallop had to be reassembled, and the long boat was taken off the deck to be used for scouting and fishing purposes.

21

MAYFLOWER II WITH REPLICA SHALLOP AND LONGBOAT

*Mayflower II with Replica
Shallop and Long Boat*

After two explorations on Cape Cod that yielded the sight of native Americans, a basket of corn and a lot of snow, they began a longer voyage in the shallop with the intent of finding a permanent place of settlement.

CORNHILL

Corn Hill Marker

"We marched to the place where we had the corn formerly, which placed we called <u>Cornhill</u>; and digged and found the rest, of which we were very glad... and sure it was God's good Providence that we found this corn, for else we know not how we should have done..."[57] Description of the Indian corn found on Cape Cod

"There was found more of their corn and of their beans of various colors; the corn and beans they brought away, purposing to give them full satisfaction when they should meet with any of them as, about some six months afterward they did, to their good content. And here is to be noted a special providence of God, and a great mercy to this poor people, that here they got seed to plant them corn the next year, or else they might have starved."[58] Bradford describing the intent of the Pilgrims to pay for the corn

On December 6 and 7, a Wednesday and Thursday, they set sail along the inner coast of Cape Cod and explored. After sleeping on shore the night of the 7th, they rose early to have their morning prayers. While having their devotions and time of prayer, they were attacked by Nauset Indians, but amazingly, none were hurt.

23

FIRST ENCOUNTER BEACH

First Encounter Beach

"About five o'clock in the morning we began to be stirring... After prayer we prepared ourselves for breakfast, and for a journey... As it fell, the water not being high enough, they laid the things down upon the shore, and came up to breakfast. Anon, all upon a sudden, we heard a great and strange cry... One of our company, being abroad, came running in, and cried, 'They are men! Indians! Indians!' And withal their arrows came flying amongst us. Our men ran out with all speed to recover their arms; as by the good providence of God they did... So after we had given God thanks for our deliverance, we took our shallop and went on our journey, and called this place The First Encounter.''[59] Bradford describing the first encounter with Native Americans

Continuing their journey by boat (shallop), it began to rain, sleet and snow on that Friday as they attempted to look for any place along the coast with a harbor. The snow may have blinded them from Barnstable Harbor where some of the Nauset Indians lived who had attacked them earlier. Then, towards evening, the rudder and mast of the shallop broke, and they attempted to steer to the nearest safe place of landing. By this time they were entering Plymouth Harbor, and sighted Clark's Island.

CLARK'S ISLAND

Clark's Island from a distance

" As we drew near, the gale being stiff, and we bearing great sail to get in, split our mast in three pieces, and were like to have cast away our shallop. Yet, by God's mercy, recovering ourselves, we had the flood with us, and struck into the harbor... Yet still the Lord kept us, and we bare up for an island before us... dark night

growing upon is, it pleased the Divine Providence that we fell upon a place of sandy ground... and coming upon a strange island, kept our watch all night in the rain... And in the morning, we marched about it, and found no inhabitants at all; and here we made our rendezvous all that day, being Saturday."[60] Bradford describing the Pilgrims landing on Clark's Island

That Saturday (December 9), they dried their clothes, repaired the shallop, and prepared to continue their exploration. The Pilgrims would not explore on Sunday, their Sabbath, in honor of the fourth commandment. Instead, they held the first church service on land near a large rock known as Pulpit Rock.

PULPIT ROCK ON CLARK'S ISLAND

Pulpit Rock

It is always good to remember that for the Pilgrim, religious liberty always preceded civil liberty. A good way to remember this is that Pulpit Rock preceded Plymouth Rock in the landing of the Pilgrims.

Inscription on Pulpit Rock

"10th of December. On the Sabbath Day we rested."[61] Entry in Mourt's Relation for their Church Service on Clark's Island

On Monday morning, December 11 (today celebrated on the 21st due to the change in the calendar in 1752), the Pilgrims landed on what is now known as Plymouth Rock. Yet, since there is no direct mention of a rock where the Pilgrims first stepped on Monday, the 11th of December, how do we know that this is indeed their first stepping stone to Plymouth?

ORIGINAL ROCK ON A WHARF IN PLYMOUTH

Rock on Wharf
(used by permission-Pilgrim Society)

In 1741, when a wharf in Plymouth was about to be built near or on top of this rock, Elder Thomas Faunce, aged ninety five, made the three mile trip from his home to the waterfront. He was born in 1646, and lived at the same time as William Bradford and many of the original Pilgrims. He related how he had been told as a child, by his father and others, when he was about eight years old, that this indeed was the rock first stepped on by the Pilgrim fathers on that Monday, of December 11. The story of Faunce was determined to be true due to his reputation and integrity.

Thomas Faunce died in 1745, at the age of ninety-nine, having left to Plymouth and her descendants a legacy that has now become famous. In 1774, the Rock was attempted to be moved by a pulley and team of oxen to Town Square so that a liberty pole could be erected over it so men would sign up to fight for independence. The Rock split in two, and some thought this was a prophetic moment predicting our split with England! The lower part was left in its original spot, and the upper part taken to Town Square.

MOVING THE ROCK

Moving the Rock

"No New Englander who is willing to indulge his native feelings, can stand upon the rock where our ancestors set the first foot after their arrival on the American shore, without experiencing emotions very different from those which are excited by any common object of the same nature. No New Englander could be willing to have that rock buried and forgotten. Let him reason as much, as coldly and ingeniously as he pleases, he will still regard that spot with emotions wholly different from those excited by other places of equal or greater importance."[62]

THE ROCK IN FRONT OF PILGRIM HALL MUSEUM

Rock in front of Pilgrim Hall

On July 4, 1834, the upper part of the rock was moved from town square to the front of Pilgrim Hall (the oldest public museum in America), which had been constructed in 1824. On its way, it fell off its cart and split in two again! The two upper portions were enjoined, and it remained surrounded by an iron fence, with the names of those who signed the Mayflower Compact inscribed nearby. At this time the date 1620 was painted on its surface.

BILLINGS CANOPY OVER PLYMOUTH ROCK

Billings Canopy

On August 2, 1859, the cornerstone for a new canopy over the bottom half of the rock was laid by Hammatt Billings. This beautiful canopy was completed in 1867. Billings was the architect of both the new canopy over the rock as well as the National Monument to the Forefathers, whose cornerstone was also laid in 1859, but not completed until 1889 (see the tour booklet entitled *Plymouth in the Words of Her Founders; the National Monument to the Forefathers*).

TERCENTENARY CANOPY OVER PLYMOUTH ROCK

Tercentenary Canopy in 1930

For the tercentenary celebration of 1920, a new canopy was erected over the Rock by the National Society of the Colonial Dames of America. This Doric column portico has remained ever since. It is interesting to note that Plymouth Rock is a unique Sienitic granite boulder, as unique to New England's coast as the Pilgrim story is in history. It is now maintained by the State of Massachusetts as an historic landmark.

PLYMOUTH ROCK

Close-up of Plymouth Rock

"Plymouth Rock does not mark a beginning or an end. It marks a revelation of that which is without beginning and without end, a purpose shining through eternity with a resplendent light, undimmed even by the imperfections of men, and a response, an answering purpose from those who oblivious, disdainful of all else, sought only an avenue for the immortal soul."[63] Remarks by Governor Calvin Coolidge at the Tercentenary Celebration

PILGRIM MOTHER MONUMENT
THE PILGRIMS CAME AS FAMILIES

Pilgrim Mother Monument

"Truly doleful was the sight of that sad and mournful parting, to see what sighs and sobs and prayers did sound amongst them, what tears did gush from every eye, and pithy speeches pierced each heart; that sundry of the Dutch strangers that stood on the quay as spectators could not refrain from tears. Yet comfortable and sweet it was to see such lively and true expressions of dear and unfeigned love."[64] Bradford relates the parting of families and church members in Holland

This monument honors mothers who came on the *Mayflower* to Plymouth. It is a monument that honors the fact that the Pilgrims migrated as twenty-four family units (totaling seventy-four of the passengers that arrived in Plymouth). William and Dorothy Bradford, like many parents, had to leave one of their sons behind in Holland. Other families left one or more members behind as well. Singles (fifteen single men and fifteen hired servants, one of whom was female) lived with a family and thus were counted as family units as well.

There is not another attempt at permanent settlement in all of history up to this time period that parallels this migration of families. Spain's attempt at colonization, or Jamestown in 1607, migrated as men only. Twelve years later, women were imported into Jamestown in order to induce men to marry and remain as families. All understood that unless the family was strong, the colony would not survive.

The solemn expression on this woman's face indicates the cost that she is willing to pay to fulfill her serious calling and responsibility as a mother to plant the foundation for a successful colony. In addition to cooking, cleaning and organizing the household, the most important task was the training of character in her children.

Cropped enlargement of her face

"Being thus constrained to leave their native soil and country... it was by many thought an adventure almost desperate; a case intolerable and a misery worse than death... Yea, though they should lose their lives in this action, yet might they have comfort in the same and their endeavors would be honorable."[65] Bradford's description of the challenges leaving England and Holland

The Bible is held firm in her hand, for it is the source from which she derives her courage and resolve and the guide to her personal relationship with God. In its pages she finds hope, and its lessons form the basis for the teachings she will give her children and the maintenance of proper relationships with other families. Discipline in the household is firm. Nothing short of unquestioned obedience is expected from her children. She believes that the character of her children will determine the character of the colony and its relationships with one another.

Cropped enlargement of the Bible

"First, as we are daily to renew our repentance with our God, especially for our sins known, and generally for our unknown trespasses... next after this heavenly peace with God and our own consciences, we are carefully to provide for peace with all men what in us lieth, especially with our associates."[66] John Robinson's counsel to Pilgrim families departing from Holland

The names of the women on the back of the monument are twenty-nine in number. Eighteen are married, ten are children, and one is a female servant. Three of the women listed got on board the *Mayflower* pregnant with child. Elizabeth

Hopkins gave birth to Oceanus halfway across the ocean. Oceanus lived at least until after 1623, but died prior to 1627. Mary Allerton gave birth to a stillborn in Provincetown harbor. Susannah White gave birth to Peregrine in Provincetown harbor. He became the last surviving passenger of the *Mayflower*, dying in 1704 at eigthty-four years of age!

WOMEN OF THE MAYFLOWER

Women listed on the Shaft

The first winter was devastating, with over half the Pilgrims dying. Fourteen of the twenty-nine women (or 48%) died the first winter. Four whole families were wiped out. Only four families went through the winter without losing a loved one. The remaining sixteen families lost at least one individual that first winter.

At the tercentenary celebration of 1920-21, the National Society Daughters of the American Revolution erected this monument: *"in memory of the heroic Women of the Mayflower."* The inscription placed on the base beneath the list of female names indicates an interpretation for the fact that this monument is a fountain. The Pilgrims believed that the family was the fountain of society, and thus must be kept pure if the nation is to be healthy.

INSCRIPTION ON THE MONUMENT

Inscription on the bottom of the Shaft

"They brought up their families in sturdy virtue and a living faith in God without which nations perish."

THE SARCOPHAGUS MONUMENT
THE FIRST WINTER

Sarcophagus Monument

"But that which was most sad and lamentable was, that in two or three months' time half of their company died, especially in January and February, being the depth of winter, and wanting houses and other comforts; being infected with the scurvy and other diseases which this long voyage and their inaccomodate condition had brought upon them. So as there died some times two or three of a day in the foresaid time, that of one hundred and odd persons, scarce fifty remained. And of these, in the time of most distress, there was but six or seven sound persons who to their great commendations, be it spoken, spared no pains night nor day, but with abundance of toil and hazard of their own health, fetched them wood, made them fires, dressed them meat, made their beds, washed their loathsome clothes, clothed and un-clothed them. In a word, did all the homely and necessary offices for them which dainty and queasy stomachs cannot endure to hear named; and all this willingly and cheerfully, without any grudging in the least, showing herein their true love unto their friends and brethren; a rare example and worthy to be remembered."[67]

38

The Sarcophagus monument lies on Cole's Hill, named after John Cole who died in Plymouth in 1725. The town maintained ownership of this property until 1855, when the Pilgrim Society became its owner. Then, in 1993, the Pilgrim

Society deeded it into the custody of the State of Massachusetts, which maintains the grounds today. Not until 1735 did anyone pay much attention to this hill overlooking the landing place of the Pilgrims.

While the Great Awakening was going on in New England, opening up the hearts of people to the God of their forefathers, a heavy rainstorm in 1735 produced a river of water down Middle Street; rushing over Cole's hill. At the end of the storm, the river had uncovered the bones of several skeletons. Upon further examination, it was concluded that these indeed were the bones of the Pilgrims who died the first winter.

In 1809 a human skull was also found, and in 1855, workmen uncovered five skeletons while digging a trench for water pipes. No coffins had been used, indicating a burial during winter. The graves were obviously unmarked, and this suggested probable burial at night. All eyes began to turn once again to ponder the sacrifice of our forefathers, half of whom died during the first winter in Plymouth.

This sacrifice of life for the cause of religious liberty deserved a memorial. In 1867, the bones discovered to that point were put in the top part of the Forefathers' Rock Canopy designed by Hammatt Billings. In 1879, more bones were discovered, and in 1883, a large tablet was placed on the hill with these words inscribed upon it:

"On this hill the Pilgrims who died the first winter were buried. This tablet marks the spot where lies the body of one found October 8, 1883. The body of another found on the 27th of the following month lies 8 feet northwest of the westerly corner of this tone. Erected 1884."

This tablet was removed in 1917 when Cole's Hill was relandscaped for the Tercentenary Celebration. In 1920, the General Society of *Mayflower* Descendants constructed the Sarcophagus Monument to house the bones of the Pilgrims. It was formerly dedicated September 8, 1921. Inside, within a waterproof casket is a plain pine box which houses many of the bones unearthed on this hill.

Why did the Pilgrims bury their dead in unmarked graves at night? The answer is simple. They did not know the disposition of the native Americans who lived nearby. They did not want them to know how weak they were, and thus buried their loved ones at night in unmarked graves to the north of the common house built at the foot of Leyden Street. Inscriptions on the two sides of the monument describe the significance of this monument.

North side of monument

"The Bones of the Pilgrims found at various times in and near this enclosure and preserved for many years in the canopy over the Rock were returned at the time of the Tercentenary celebration and are deposited within this monument. Erected by the General Society of Mayflower Descendants, A.D. 1920. " Inscription on North side of the Monument

41

South side of monument

"About a hundred sowls came over in this first ship and began this work which God in His Goodness hath hithertoe Blesed: Let His Holy Name have ye praise – Bradford, 1650. " Inscription on South side of the Monument

On the east (or back of the monument), a list of the forty-six men, women and children who died the first winter are listed after the opening line, "Of the One Hundred and Four passengers these died in Plymouth during the first year."

WEST FACING INSCRIPTION

Western Face

"This Monument marks the First Burying Ground in Plymouth of the Passengers of the Mayflower. Here, under cover of darkness, the fast dwindling company laid their dead, levelling the earth above them lest the Indians should know how many were the graves. Reader! History records no nobler venture for faith and freedom than that of this Pilgrim band. In weariness and painfulness, in watchings, often in hunger and cold they laid the foundations of a state wherein every man, through countless ages, should have liberty to worship God in his

own way. May their example inspire thee to do thy part in perpetuating and spreading the lofty ideas of our republic throughout the world!"

What example ought we to follow? It was said by Jesus Christ, the author of the Christian religion to which the Pilgrims ascribed so fervently, that "greater love hath no man than this, that a man lay down his life for his friends."[68] The testimony that follows in Bradford's own words give us the excellent example to follow:

"... As this calamity fell among the passengers that were to be left here to plant, and were hasted ashore and made to drink water that the seamen might have the more beer, and one in his sickness desiring but a small can of beer, it was answered that if he were their own father he should have none... the disease began to fall amongst them also... they that before had been boon companions in drinking and jollity in the time of their health and welfare, began now to desert one another in this calamity, saying they would not hazard their lives for them, they should be infected by coming to help them in their cabins; and so, after they came to lie by it, would do little or nothing for them but, 'if they died, let them die.' But such of the passengers as were yet aboard showed them what mercy they could, which made some of their hearts relent, as the boatswain (and some others)

who was a proud young man and would often curse and scoff at the passengers. But when he grew weak, they had compassion on him and helped him; then he confessed he did not deserve it at their hands, he had abused them in word and deed. 'Oh' (saith he), 'you, I see, show your love like Christians indeed one to another, but we let one another lie and die like dogs.' Another lay cursing his wife, saying if it had not been for her he had never come on this unlucky voyage..."[69]

MASSASOIT MONUMENT
PILGRIM RELATIONS WITH THE INDIANS

Massasoit Monument

"In his person he is a very lusty man, in his best years, an able body, grave of countenance, and spare of speech. In his attire little or nothing differing from the rest of his followers, only in a great chain of white bone heads about his neck, and at it behind his neck hangs a little bag of tobacco, which he drank and gave us to drink; his face was painted with a sad red like murry, and oiled both head and face...."[70] Pilgrim description of Massasoit at Peace Treaty

45

Massasoit

Standing near the Sarcophagus monument is a grand statue of Massasoit, chief of the Wompanoag Indians. Constructed by the Improved Order of Red Men and the Daughters of Pocahontas, it was placed on its pedestal on September 3, 1921 and dedicated September 5, 1921. The sculptor of this statue was Cyrus E. Dallin of Arlington, Massachusetts, who lived as a boy with Indian playmates and always admired their qualities of character. From the voyage of Columbus through to the early 1600s, the white man's relationship with the native American (whether north or south) was not always positive. Faults lie on both sides for sure. However, the relations of the Pilgrims with the native Americans here in Plymouth is a tribute to both these Englishmen and the native Americans on these shores.

One of the most amazing aspects of the relations of the Pilgrims with the Indians was their introduction to Samoset and Squanto which paved the way for their friendly relationship with Massasoit.

"But about the 16th of March, a certain Indian came boldly amongst them and spoke to them in broken English, which they could well understand but marveled at it. At length they understood

by discourse with him, that he was not of these parts, but belonged to the eastern parts where some English ships came to fish, with whom he was acquainted and could name sundry of them by their names, amongst whom he had got his language. He became profitable to them in acquainting them with many things concerning the state of the country in the east parts where he lived, which was afterwards profitable unto them; as also of the people here, of their names, number and strength, of their situation and distance from this place, and who was chief amongst them. His name was Samoset. He told them also of another Indian whose name was Squanto, a native of this place, who had been in England and could speak better English than himself."[71] Bradford describing their first visit from Samoset in 1621

47

The story of Squanto is truly remarkable. He was the lone survivor of a plague that killed all of his tribe at Patuxet, now inhabited by the Pilgrims as new Plymouth. Before this plague however, Squanto had been captured by Thomas Hunt, who purposed to see him and other captured native Americans as slaves in Spain. Squanto escaped to England, learned English while being treated well in London, and had arrived back in his homeland only to find hardly any living relatives. His arrival was only six months to a year before the Pilgrims came! Bradford described him as "a special instrument sent of God for their good beyond all expectation."[72]

After this meeting with Samoset, and subsequent sightings of other Indians, the Pilgrims signed a Peace Treaty with the Indians in March of 1621. This concept of forming a covenant or agreement for two or more parties to be equal before the law was a concept familiar to those of the Reformation period. Their church covenant was an extension of their personal covenant with God, and their civil covenant was an extension in principle of their church covenant. Now, their covenant with the Indians, a sort of covenant with a foreign nation, was also an extension of the same concept.

48

SIGNING OF THE PEACE TREATY

Alto-Relief from Forefather's Monument

"... their great sagamore Massasoit was hard by, with Quadequina his brother, and all their men. They could not express well in English what they

*would; but after an hour the king came to the top
of a hill over against us, and had in his train sixty
men, that we could well behold them, and they
us. We were not willing to send our governor to
them, and they were unwilling to come to us. So
Squanto went again to him, who brought word
that we should send one to parley with him,
which we did, which was Edward Winslow, to
know his mind, and signify the mind and will of
our Governor, which was to have trading and
peace with him... Our messenger made a speech
unto him, that King James saluted him with
words of love and peace, and did accept of him as
his friend and ally, and that our governor desired
to see him and to truck with him, and to confirm
peace with him, as his next neighbor."*

*"They saluted him and he them... conducted him
to a house then in building, where we placed a
green rug and three or four cushions... After
salutations, our governor kissing his hand, and
the king kissed him, and so they sat down...
Then they treated or peace, which was: 1. That
neither he nor any of his should injur or do hurt
to any of our people. 2. That if any of his did
hurt to any of ours, he should send the offender,
that we might punish him. 3. That if any of our
tools were taken away when our people were at
work, he should cause them to be restored, and
if ours did any harm to any of his, we would
do the like to him. 4. If any did unjustly war
against him, we would aid him; if any did war*

*against us, he should aid us. 5. He should send
to his neighbor confederates, to certify them of
this, that they might not wrong us, but might be
likewise comprised in the condition of peace. 6.
That when their men came to us, they should
leave their bows and arrows behind them, as
we should do our pieces when we came to them.
Lastly, that doing this, King James would esteem
of him as his friend and ally. All the while he sat
by the governor, he trembled for fear.* "[73] Pilgrims
describing the Peace Treaty with Massasoit

Plaque beneath Massasoit

The inscribed tablet at the base of Massasoit
says that this Sagamore Chief was the "preserver
and protector" of the Pilgrims. Indeed this
was the truth, for without it the Pilgrims would
probably not have survived. It was a friendship
in honor of the Wompanoag as much as it was
the wisdom of the Pilgrim. Massasoit had to
overlook the past injustices from white men
and trust these Englishmen. This was no small

task. An incident that explained why the Nauset Indians had initially attacked the Pilgrims at their "first encounter" explains the challenge.

One John Billington, whose younger brother had nearly blown up the *Mayflower* in Provincetown by playing with gun powder, and whose father would be the first individual put to death for murder in 1630, was lost in the woods and picked up by the Nauset Indians. This incident occurred when the Pilgrims traveled to retrieve the boy.

"One thing was very grievous unto us at this place. There was an old woman, whom we judged to be no less than a hundred years old, which came to see us, because she never saw English; yet could not behold us without breaking forth into great passion, weeping and crying excessively. We demanding the reason of it, they told us she had three sons, who, when Master Hunt was in these parts, went aboard his ship to trade with him, and he carried them captives unto Spain, (for Tisquantum at that time was carried away also), by which means she was deprived of the company of her children in her old age. We told them we were sorry that any Englishman should give them that offense, that Hunt was a bad man, that all the English that heard of it condemned him for the same; but for us, we would not offer then any such injury, though it would gain us all the skins in the country."[74]

The trust given by both sides to each other in forming peace was commendable, and paved the way for what has come to be known as the First Thanksgiving. No one knows for sure the exact date of this three day festival patterned after the harvest feast in England and having its roots in the Feast of Tabernacles in the Jewish calendar. It could have been as early as late September when the corn harvest actually occurred. The only detailed explanation we have is from Edward Winslow's letter to a friend in England.

THE FIRST THANKSGIVING 1621

*Painting of the First Thanksgiving
(used by permission-Pilgrim Society)*

"Our harvest being gotten, our governor sent four men on fowling, that so we might, after a special manner, rejoice together after we had gathered the fruit of our labors. They four in one day killed as much fowl as, with a little help beside, served the company almost a week.

At which time, amongst other recreations, we exercised our arms, many of the Indians coming amongst us, and among the rest their greatest king, Massasoit, with some ninety men, whom for three days we entertained and feasted; and they went out and killed five deer, which they brought to the plantation, and bestowed on our governor, and upon the captain and others. And although it be not always so plentiful as it was at this time with us, yet by the goodness of God we are so far from want, that we often wish you partakers of our plenty. "[75] Winslow's description of the First Thanksgiving, 1621

In March of 1623, news came that Massasoit was sick. Edward Winslow, John Hamden and Hobbomock (the Indian who was now the Pilgrim interpreter after Squanto died in 1622), were sent by Governor Bradford to visit with him and bring him some natural herbs and medicines that Samuel Fuller had recommended.

Upon arriving to see Massasoit who was at the point of death, Edward Winslow did what he could, and the recovery was so swift that Winslow remarked, *"We with admiration blessed God for giving his blessing to such raw and ingnorant means, making no doubt of his recovery, himself and all of them acknowledging us the instruments of his preservation... Never did I see a man so low brought, recover in that measure in so short a time."[76]* After ministering to him for a few days, Massasoit remarked, *"Now I see the English are my friends and love me; and whilst I live, I will never forget this kindness they have showed me."[77]*

It is a fitting tribute to both the Wompanoags and the Pilgrims that their friendship was so amicable. The Peace Treaty lasted more than fifty years. In honor of this friendly relationship, the ceremonies of September, 1921 took place on the top of Cole's Hill for the unveiling of this grand statue. Princess Woontonekanuske, at seventy-three years of age, the only known living descendent of Massasoit by eight generations, unveiled the statue.

"The unveiling ceremonies opened with an invocation by Henry J. Walsh, which called for the response, 'Hear Us, O Great Spirit,' by all the tribes and councils with upraised hands.

P.G.S. Weeks as presiding officer introduced Mr. Dallin, the sculpture, who made delivery of the statue to the Massasoit Memorial Association and in the course of his remarks told something of his boyhood among the Indians of the West and what steadfast friends he found them. Princess Woontonekanuske, garbed in full ceremonial dress, then laid down the handsome bouquet of dahlias and advanced to the halliards securing the American flag to the statute and with a vigorous tug released them and the flag falling disclosed the fine work which had come from Mr. Dallin's hand and brain, and cheers and whoops rang out from the crowd as the figure was disclosed. As the applause died away the band played 'The Star Spangled Banner'"[78] Description of the Unveiling of the Massasoit Monument in 1921

The Massasoit statue is over ten feet tall and weighs over 1500 pounds. It is made of hollow bronze. Massasoit is looking out in the harbor, and its position and disposition is described below as it was envisioned by Dallin himself.

MASSASOIT MONUMENT

Massasoit close-up

"Mr. Dallin described the position of the figure as representing the moment when Massasoit first described the Mayflower *coming in by the Gurnet at the entrance to his harbor. He has stepped on the rock for a better point of vantage and gazes seaward at the approaching ship, which he realizes is bringing white men here to the lands over which he is the ruler. The face of the statue is strong and is described well as that of one would make a staunch friend or a good enemy."[79]* Description of Massasoit Monument and its Sculptor's Intent

THE BRADFORD MONUMENT
PILGRIM GOVERNOR AND HISTORIAN

Bradford Monument

"From my years in days of youth,
God did make known to me his truth.
And call'd me from my native place,
For to enjoy the means of grace.
In wilderness he did me guide,
And in strange lands for me provide.
In fears and wants, through weal and woe,
A pilgrim, passed I to and fro:
Oft left of them whom I did trust;
How vain it is to rest on dust!
A man of sorrows I have been,
And many dangers I have seen
Wars, wants, peace, plenty, have I known;
And some advanc'd, others thrown down.
The humble poor, cheerful glad;
Rich, discontent, sower and sad.
When fears and sorrows have been mixt,
Consolations came betwixt.
Faint not, poor soul, in God still trust,

Fear not the things thou suffer must;
For, whom he loves he doth chastise,
and Then all tears wipes from their eyes.
Farewell, dear children, whom I love,
Your better Father is above;
When I am gone, he can supply;
To him I leave you when I die.
Fear him in truth, walk in his ways,
And he will bless you all your days.
My days are spent, old age is come,
My strength it fails, my glass near run.
Now I will wait, when work is done,
Until my happy change shall come,
When from my labors I shall rest,
With Christ above for to be blest."[80]

Autobiographical Poem by William Bradford

Although the Bradford monument was also made by Dallin and designed for the 300th anniversary of the Pilgrims' landing, like most of the others on the waterfront, it was not completed and placed on its pedestal until Thanksgiving day, 1976 in commemoration of the bicentennial of the Declaration of Independence. The monument depicts a close to life-size statute of William Bradford, governor and historian of the Plymouth. Excerpts from *Of Plymouth Plantation*, written by Bradford, adorn its sides.

William Bradford was born in 1590, in Austerfield, England. His parents died while he was very young. His grandparents, and then his uncle and aunt, began an education for William in farming. He soon became sick, so that between the ages of seven and eleven, he rarely left his bed. Bradford would later say that this sickness was sent by the Providence of God because it kept him from the *"vanities of youth."* When he was twelve years old, he began to read the Scriptures, and it had such an effect upon him that he yearned to hear it explained.

This brought him into contact with the preaching of Richard Clyfton in Babworth, several miles distant from his home. Soon he became converted to the Christian faith, seeing the "errors" of the English church, and joining the movement known as the "separatists." After a dedicated time of prayer and study of the Scriptures, young William became attached to the Separatist church, then meeting in Babworth. This attachment brought on the scorn and mockery of his uncles, as well as his neighbors. At about age fourteen, he was disowned, and taken in by William Brewster in Scrooby, not far from his home. However, before he left at this tender age, he clearly let all his relatives and friends know his convictions and intentions:

BRADFORD MONUMENT

Bradford Monument close-up

"Were I like to endanger my life, or consume my estate by any ungodly courses, your counsels to me were very seasonable; but you know that I have been diligent and provident in my calling, and not only desirous to augment what I have, but also to enjoy it in your company, to part from which will be as great a cross as can befall me. Nevertheless, to keep a good conscience, and walk in such a way as God has prescribed in his Word, is a thing which I must prefer before you all, and above life itself. Wherefore, since 'tis for a good cause that I am like to suffer the disasters which you lay before me, you have no cause to be either angry with me; yea, I am not only willing to part with every thing that is dear to me in this world for this cause, but I am also thankful that God has given me an heart to do, and will accept me so to suffer for him."[81] William Bradford's confession before his relatives at age 14

As a teenager of barely sixteen, he joined the Separatist church that met in secret at Scrooby Manor, the home of William Brewster. At age eighteen, along with many of the other separatist Pilgrims, he was betrayed and put in jail in Boston, England for attempting to go to Holland. At age nineteen, he suffered near shipwreck on the voyage to Holland. Finally, along with the others, they did make it to Amsterdam for a year, and then to Leyden for eleven more years. Here he married Dorothy, and became a pillar in the church under the leadership of John Robinson.

He came to the new world on the *Mayflower* after barely turning thirty, lost his wife who drowned in Provincetown harbor, and nearly lost his own when the common house almost burned to the ground. He then found himself unanimously elected the second governor of Plymouth after the untimely death of the revered John Carver. Thus, in the spring of 1621, William Bradford began a career of leading the Plymouth colony almost without interruption until his death in 1657, at the age of sixty-seven.

Bradford was a calm and courageous leader who governed by the law. When given full control and ownership of the colony through the Pierce Patent in 1621, he promptly turned the power back to the people under the previous document of the Mayflower Compact of 1620. He was also compassionate, taking in orphans whose parents died, having been an orphan himself.

William Bradford was also a scholar. He studied Hebrew by candlelight in the new world, but had already mastered Latin, Dutch, French and the Greek of the New Testament. He became proficient in Antiquity, Philosophy and Theology. Throughout his life, he demonstrated that one could teach himself when no formal education was available.

Bradford was an historian, and largely due to this we know the details about the Pilgrims and their settlement here in the new world. Beginning in the year 1630, he began to compile a history of this Pilgrim band, and continued it until just prior to his death. Called at times the "Log of the Mayflower", but called by Bradford *Of Plymouth Plantation*, it gives details of the life of the Pilgrims from the late 1500s through the year 1647. It is wrtten in classical style, and is rightfully considered the first American classic written on these shores.

OF PLYMOUTH PLANTATION

Original Manuscript Facsimile

"After looking at the volume and reading the records on the flyleaf, I said, 'My lord, I am going to say something which you may think rather audacious. I think this book ought to go back to Massachusetts.'"[82] Request of Senator Hoar to the Bishop of London in 1896

"Well, I didn't know you cared anything about it." Response to Senator Hoar by the Bishop of London

"I do not think many Americans will gaze upon it without a little trembling of the lips and a little gathering of mist in the eyes, as they think of the story of suffering, of sorrow, of peril, of exile, of death and of lofty triumph which that book tells —which the hand of the great leader and founder of America has traced on those pages…"[83] Remarks Senator Hoar on the return of the Bradford Manuscript

This Bradford classic has a story almost as remarkable as Bradford and the Pilgrims themselves. Having been passed down to his children, it was borrowed by historians and went through fires and floods, only to find itself being taken a booty by the British in the evacuation of Boston in 1776. Finding its way to the Bishop of London's personal library, it was rediscovered and published just before the Civil War (by the Massachusetts Historical Society, 1853).

Senator Hoar of Massachusetts set eyes on it in 1896, and desiring to bring it back to Massachusetts, asked the bold question of the London dignitary. The famous reply echoed deep in his heart and in a sense revealed the lack of attention to our own heritage when it was stated, *"I didn't know you cared anything about it."*[84] The first Massachusetts edition was published in 1898, with a reprint in 1901 made available to the public in America after the original was returned. Updated editions with excellent footnotes are now available at Pilgrim Hall Museum.

BREWSTER GARDENS
THE LIFE OF WILLIAM BREWSTER

Brewster Garden Sign
And Town Brook

"We came to a conclusion, by most voices, to set on the mainland... on a high ground, where there is a great deal of land cleared...and there is a very sweet brook runs under the hill side, and many delicate springs of as good water as can be drunk, and we may harbor our shallops and boats exceeding well, and in this brook much good fish in their seasons."[85] Description by the Pilgrims of what is now Brewster Gardens

W hen the Pilgrims decided to settle in what is now Plymouth, they did so for good reasons. They needed four things in order to make a permanent settlement. First, they wanted a hill so that they could defend themselves if needed. Second, they wanted a brook in which they could fish as well as safely harbor their shallops. Third, they desired land that was at least partially cleared for planting crops. Fourth, they desired fresh water which would necessitate the existence of a spring. The place now called Brewster Gardens and its surroundings had all four of these characteristics.

TOWN BROOK FROM COURT STREET

66

The original town brook was much wider than the one seen in Plymouth today. The waterfront has changed significantly since the tercentenary celebration in 1920-21. It was also at this time that the land now called Brewster Gardens was set aside in memory of the Pilgrims. Mrs. William Forbes of Milton, in cooperation with the town of Plymouth, set aside this little park in memory of the Pilgrims in general, and William Brewster in particular.

Mrs. Forbes' mother was the wife of Ralph Waldo Emerson and a Plymouth girl. It was called Brewster Gardens at the suggestion of

Mrs. Forbes due to the fact that most of the land on the south side was originally owned by William Brewster as his fields in the early 1620's. Since there was no easy access from Leyden Street when the Plymouth County Gas and Electric Company occupied the spot, a set of stairs was laid into the hillside which exist to this day.

PILGRIM MAID

Pilgrim Maid Monument

"To those intrepid English women whose courage, fortitude, and devotion brought a new nation into being, this statue of the Pilgrim maiden is dedicated." Inscription on the plaque in front of the pool

In 1924 the National Society of New England Women erected the statue of the Pilgrim Maiden. It was placed on a boulder from Rocky Nook. The maiden looks down on a pool of water overflowing from the Brewster spring, commemorating the single women, children and servants who came here in 1620 with such courage and fortitude. It was unusual enough for women who were married to travel on such a voyage in the early 1600s, but the challenge to single women and female children was even greater! The maiden stands firm against the winds of adversity as she clutches a Bible firmly in her hand.

Pilgrim Maid

A permanent Town Brook Committee, under the direction of Dr. Helen Pierce carried on the work of improving the appearance of these gardens. In 1959 the Plymouth County Electric Company gave its land at the corner of Leyden Street to the town. Another lot was given to the town by its owner, Mr. John D. Luddy of Windsor, Connecticut in 1968. A final strip of land behind the post office was sold by the Federal government for $1 in the same year. Also in 1968, the Plymouth Park Commission under the direction of Mr. Walter Haskell joined with the Pilgrim Society in placing a memorial boulder to Elder Brewster near the entrance that faces the waterfront.

BREWSTER STONE

Brewster Stone

"...A man that had done and suffered much for ye Lord Jesus and ye gospells sake ...he was qualified above many, he was wise and discreete and well spoken ...of a very cherfull spirite ...under valuing him self and his own abilities."
Inscription on the stone is taken from Bradford

William Brewster served as Elder of the Pilgrim church, since their pastor, John Robinson, did not accompany them on their journey, but instead stayed behind to lead the church left in Holland. He had been post-master general in Scrooby for the Queen of England along the Great North Road from London to Scotland. He risked much to join with the Separatists, and it was appreciated, especially so by William Bradford, since had lived with him as a teenager in England. The following are tributes to William Brewster by Bradford.

"But now removing into this country all these things were laid aside again, and a new course of living must be framed unto, in which he was no way unwilling to take his part, and to bear his burthen with the rest, living many times without bread or corn many months together, having many times nothing but fish and often wanting that also; and drunk nothing but water for many years together, yea till within five or six years of his death. And yet he lived by the blessing of God in health till very old age. And besides that, he would labor with his hands in the fields as long as he was able. Yet when the church had no other minister, he taught twice every Sabbath, and that both powerfully and profitably, to the great contentment of the hearers and their comfortable edification; yea, many were brought to God by his ministry... He was wise and discreet and well spoken, having a grave and deliberate utterance, of a very cheerful spirit, very sociable and pleasant amongst his friends, of an humble

and modest mind, of a peaceable disposition, undervaluing himself and his own abilities and sometimes overvaluing others.

"Inoffensive and innocent in his life and conversation, which gained him the love of those without as well as those within; yet he would tell them plainly of their faults and evils, both publicly and privately, but in such a manner as usually was well taken from him. He was tenderhearted and compassionate of such as were in misery, but especially of such as had been of good estate and rank and were fallen into want and poverty either for goodness and religion's sake or by the injury and oppression of others; he would say of all men these deserved to be pitied most. And none did more offend and displease him than such as would haughtily and proudly carry and lift up themselves, being risen from nothing and having little else in them to command them but a few clothes or a little riches more than others."

71

"In teaching, he was very moving and stirring of affections, also very plain and distinct in what he taught; by which means he became the more profitable to the hearers. He had a singular good gift in prayer, both public and private, in ripping up the heart and conscience before God in the humble confession of sin, and begging the mercies of God in Christ for the pardon of the same. He always thought it were better for

ministers to pray oftener and special occasions as in days of humiliation and the like. His reason was that the heart and spirits of all, especially the weak, could hardly continue and stand bent as it were so long towards God as they ought to do in that duty, without flagging and falling off."[86]

LEYDEN STREET
THE FIRST STREET OF THE PLANTATION

Leyden Street to the Hill

"Thursday, the 28ᵗʰ of December, so many as could went to work on the hill where we purposed to build our platform for our ordnance, and which doth command all the plain and the bay, and from whence we may see far into the sea, and might be easier impaled, having two rows of houses and a fair street. So in the afternoon we went to measure out the grounds, and first we

took notice how many families there were, willing all single men that had no wives to join with some family, as they thought fit, that so we might build fewer houses, which was done, and we reduced them to nineteen families. To greater families we allotted larger plots, to every person half a pole in breadth, and three in length, and so lots were cast where every man should lie, which was done, and staked out... we agreed that every man should build his own house, thinking that by that course men would make more haste than working in common. The common house, in which for the first winter we made our rendezvous, being near finished, wanted only covering, it being about twenty feet square. Some should make mortar, and some greater thatch, so that in four days half of it was thatched." [87] Description of Laying out the First Street of the Plantation

Fair Street

When the Pilgrims decided to settle in what is now Plymouth, they named their main street First Street. It was later changed to Leyden, or "fair street", after the town the Pilgrims had resided in for eleven years in Holland. A replica common house stood for a short time in 1921 on Leyden Street, within the confines of Brewster Gardens. Now, a plaque on the south side of Leyden Street coming from the waterfront (on the first building) commemorates the first house built by the Pilgrims.

COMMON HOUSE PLAQUE

Common House Plaque

"This tablet is erected by the Commonwealth of Massachusetts to mark the site of the first house built by the Pilgrims. In that house on the 21st of February 1621 (New Style) the right of popular suffrage was exercised and Myles Standish was chosen Captain by a majority vote. On or near this spot, April 1, 1621, the memorable treaty with Massasoit was made."

"...and the 25th day (of December) began to erect the first house for common use to receive them and their goods."88

"...in the morning we called a meeting for the establishing of military orders among ourselves, and we chose Miles Standish our captain, and gave authority of command in affairs."89

The Pilgrims did not celebrate Christmas Day, since its date of December 25 was to them more Roman than Biblical. On the 25th of December, 1621, Bradford called everyone out to work as usual, with no special holiday celebration. Some objected saying "it went against their conscience to work on that day." When finding that those same individuals were at play instead of devotion, "he went to them and took away their implements and told them that was against his conscience, that they should play and others work."

This plaque also commemorates the Peace Treaty signed with Massasoit in the Common house then under construction: *"they saluted him and he them... conducted him to a house then in building, where we placed a green rug and three or four cushions... After salutations, our governor kissing his hand, and the king kissed him, and so they sat down... Then they treated of peace."*[90]

As one walks up Leyden street, on the right hand side there is a plaque marking the spot (on the side of a house) where Dr. Samuel Fuller lived.

SAMUEL FULLER PLAQUE

Samuel Fuller Plaque

"This spot bounded by Middle or King St. And LeBaron Alley once owned by Dr. Samuel Fuller of the Mayflower, *was given by his wife and son to the First church for the use of the minister."*
Inscription on plaque

When John Endicott became governor of Salem in 1628, he wrote to William Bradford, asking them to send Doctor Samuel Fuller, because many were dying like they had in Plymouth. Samuel Fuller did go that winter, and did more than cure their diseases, for he preached on that which had separated the Pilgrim from the Puritan – the outward form of God's worship – from the church service to government. Endicott wrote to Bradford stating:

"I acknowledge myself much bound to you for your kind love and care in sending Mr. Fuller among us, and rejoice much that I am by him satisfied touching your judgment of the outward form of God's worship."[91] Continuing up the right hand side one can find a stone marker commemorating the place where John Howland's house once stood.

JOHN HOWLAND'S STONE

John Howland's Stone

"On this spot stood the First House of the Mayflower Pilgrim John Howland. The Pilgrim John Howland Society 1978." Inscription

After falling overboard on the voyage, and miraculously being saved, John Howland became a good member of church and community! His gravestone in Burial Hill is marked with the testimony of the records of Plymouth that he lived to be the last male Pilgrim who came over on the *Mayflower*!

(At the intersection of Main Street a marker on the left indicates the Brewster home and the location of the famous Spring.)

BREWSTER SPRING MARKER

Brewster Spring Marker

Pilgrim Spring on the meerstead set off to Elder William Brewster in the original allotment December 1620." Inscription on the top of the marker

"*... and there is a very sweet brook runs under the hill side, and many delicate springs of as good water as can be drunk...* "[92]

(Across the intersection there is another plaque marking the place where William Bradford's home once stood.)

BRADFORD PLAQUE

Bradford Plaque

In 1627, an eye-witness account was given by Isaack de Rasieres, a Dutch trader, indicating the layout of the original Plymouth Plantation. It is for this reason that the living museum, Plymouth Plantation, portrays life in the year 1627 and affords so many tourists a delightful visit to the past when the Pilgrims dwelled in this town.

Intersection of Town

"New Plymouth lies on the slope of a hill stretching east towards the sea-coast, with a broad street about a cannon shot of 800 feet long, leading down the hill; with a street crossing in the middle, northwards to the rivulet and southwards to the land. The houses are constructed of clapboards, with gardens also enclosed behind and at the sides with clapboards, so that their houses and courtyards are arranged in good order, with a stockade against sudden attack; and at the ends of the streets there are three wooden gates. In the center, on the cross street, stands the Governor's house, before which is a square stockade upon which four patereros are mounted, so as to enfilade the streets."[93]

BURIAL HILL
The Pilgrim Meeting House and Fort

Burial Hill Sign

Fort Sign

"This summer they built a fort with good timber, both strong and comely... it served them also for a meeting house and was fitted accordingly for that use."[94] Bradford's description of the Fort and Meeting House

Cannon Site (with grate)

"...whereas we have a hill, called The Mount, inclosed within our pale, under which our town is seated; we resolved to erect a Fort thereon; from whence a few might easily secure the town from any assault...and though it took the greatest part of our strength from dressing our corn, yet, life being continued, we hoped God would raise some means instead thereof, for our further preservation."[95] Winslow's description of the building of the Fort in 1622

82

"Upon the hill they have a large square house, with a flat roof, built of thick sawn planks stayed with oak beams, upon the top of which they have six cannon, which shoot iron balls of four and five pounds, and command the surrounding country. The lower part they use for their church, where they preach on Sundays and the usual holidays."[96]

Town Square with Two Churches

At the top of the hill, behind the stone church (now Unitarian) built in 1897, is Burial Hill. To the right of this church is the Church of the Pilgrimage, begun after the 1801 Unitarian controversy (a Congregational church and trinitarian in doctrine). If one would climb the stairs, they would find the marker indicating the place of the Pilgrim fort and first meeting house (where they held their church services). The fort was built in 1622, including a diamond shaped stockade fence to protect from sudden attack. The hill was called Fort Hill until 1698. In 1633, 1635 and 1642, the fort was repaired and the stockade enlarged. Even a watch tower was built. Two ancient cannon from the general time period once graced the hillside.

PILGRIM PROGRESS
THE PILGRIM CHURCH SERVICE

The Pilgrim Progress

"... They assemble by beat of drum, each with his musket or firelock, in front of the captain's door; they have their cloaks on, and place themselves in order, three abreast, and are led by a sergeant without beat of drum. Behind comes the Governor, in a long robe; beside him on the right hand, comes the preacher with his cloak on, and on the left hand, the captain with his side-arms and cloak on, and with a small cane in his hand, and so they march in good order, each sets his arms down near him."[97] Isaack DeRasiers describing the Pilgrims going to Church in 1627

The Pilgrims would worship on Sunday mornings from about 9 o'clock in the morning until Noon. This service would be simple, consisting of almost an hour of psalm singing, an offering for the poor as well as the needs of those who ministered, and then a two hour sermon.

They would then eat a prepared lunch (honoring the Sabbath by preparing it the day before), and have another Sabbath meeting for about three hours. In this afternoon service, testimonies from heads of households as to how they would apply what they heard in the morning would often take place.

A PILGRIM CHURCH SERVICE

The Pilgrims Going to Church

"With arms they gathered in the congregation to worship Almighty God. But they were armed, that in peace they might seek divine guidance in righteousness; not that they might prevail by force, but that they might do right though they perished."[98] Remarks by Governor Calvin Coolidge, December 21, 1920

The Pilgrims remained without a pastor until 1629. However, their memory of the ministry of their pastor in Holland, John Robinson, stayed with them. His death in 1625 was a difficult blow since many had believed he would join them at some point in the future. It is a testimony to the kind of teaching they received that a congregation under this kind of pressure would remain intact and in unity for this long without the direct involvement of their pastor.

On Burial Hill, as it is now called, Pilgrims were presumably buried after the first winter. Wooden markers were used but did not survive. We only know of Bradford's grave due to the fact that his son William desired to be buried next to his father.

86

BRADFORD'S GRAVE

Bradford's grave marker

"He was a person for study as well as action; and hence, notwithstanding the difficulties

through which he passed in his youth, attained unto a notable skill in languages; the Dutch tongue was become almost a vernacular to him as the English; the French tongue he could also manage; the Latin and the Greek he had mastered; but the Hebrew he most of all studied, 'Because,' he said, 'he would see with his own eyes the ancient oracles of God in their native beauty.' He was also well skilled in History, Antiquity, and in Philosophy; and for Theology he became so versed in it... but the crown of all was his holy, prayerful, watchful, and fruitful walk with God, where in he was very exemplary."

"At length he fell into an indisposition of body, which rendred him unealthy for a whole winter; and as the spring advanced, his health yet more declined; yet he felt himself not what he counted sick, till one day; in the night after which, the God of heaven so filled his mind with ineffable consolations, that he seemed little short of Paul, rapt up unto the unutterable entertainments of Paradise. The next morning he told his friends, 'That the good Spirit of God had given him a pledge of his happiness in another world, and the first-fruits of his eternal glory;' and on the day following he died, May 9, 1657, in the 69th year of his age —lamented by all the colonies of New-England, as a common blesing and father to them all.'[99] Cotton Mather's *Life of William Bradford*

1 Plymouth Plantation
2 Howland House
3 Harlow House
4 Jenny Grist Mill
5 Sparrow House
6 First Church
7 Burial Hill
8 1749 Courthouse
9 Wm. Bradford Statue
10 Plymouth Rock
11 Coles Hill
12 Mayflower II
13 Ply. Wax Museum
14 Sponner House
15 Mayflower Society
16 Pilgrim Hall Museum
17 Hedge House
18 Memorial Hall
19 Pilgrim Mother Statue
20 Massasoit Statue
21 Pilgrim Maiden Statue
22 Sarcophagus
23 Forefathers' Monument
24 Taylor Trask Museum
25 Post Office

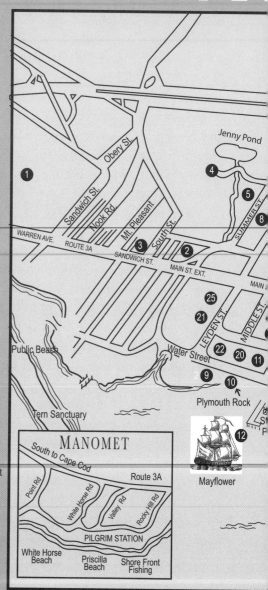

Jenny Pond

Obery St.
Sandwich St.
Nook Rd.
Mt. Pleasant
South St.
Summer St.

WARREN AVE.
ROUTE 3A
SANDWICH ST.
MAIN ST. EXT.
MAIN

Public Beach

Water Street
LEYDEN ST.
MIDDLE ST.

Tern Sanctuary

Plymouth Rock

MANOMET
South to Cape Cod
Route 3A
Point Rd.
White Horse Rd.
Valley Rd.
Rocky Hill Rd.
PILGRIM STATION
White Horse Beach
Priscilla Beach
Shore Front Fishing

Mayflower

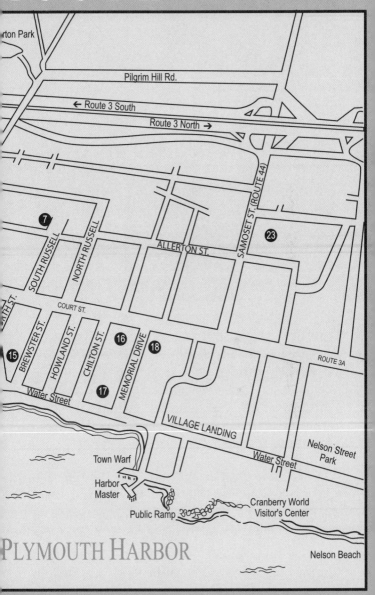

PART TWO

THE FOREFATHERS' MONUMENT

National Monument to the Forefathers

"We come in our prosperity to remember your trials; and here on the spot where New England began to be, we come to learn of our pilgrim fathers a deep and lasting lesson of virtue, enterprise, patience, zeal, and faith!"[1] Edward Everett at the Dedication of Pilgrim Hall Museum, 1824

Begun with a gift in 1794, during the administration of George Washington, and dedicated in 1889, and spanning nearly a century, *Forefathers' Monument* is one of the longest projects from conception to completion in memory of our national history! Located on

Allerton Street, and standing eigthy-one feet tall, the National Monument to the Forefathers is acknowledged to be the largest solid granite monument in the United States.

Joseph Coolidge inspired the idea by giving one guinea to start a fund to erect a monument in memory of the Pilgrims in 1794. Thirty years later, in 1824, a Mr. Bradford remembered this fund at the dedication of Pilgrim Hall, the oldest public museum in the United States.

PILGRIM HALL MUSEUM

Pilgrim Hall Museum

89

In addition to the construction of a museum building, the Pilgrim Society had in its charter of 1820 the *"...procuring in the town of Plymouth a suitable lot or piece of ground for the erection of a monument to perpetuate the history of the virtues, the enterprise and unparalleled sufferings of their ancestors who first settled in that ancient town...."*[2] Charter of the Pilgrim Society, 1820

Twenty-five years later, in 1849, a plan was constructed to actually raise the necessary funds and erect a monument. A large celebration was held in 1853. A processional parade, together with ceremonies and speeches produced a holiday on Monday, August 1. Over 2,500 people attended the dinner celebration alone. The five hour ceremony of speeches, hymns and poems was described in this way: *"The throng of people was immense, but the crowd, which seemed to be animated by one soul, was as still and orderly as a Sabbath congregation..."*[3]

HAMMATT BILLINGS

Hammatt Billings

"As a designer on wood he is without a rival in this country... we know of no one who draws so many things so well... perhaps his forte is in the drawing and grouping of the human figure. All his figures have a naturalness and correctness on whatever scale they are drawn... He conceives his design so clearly and distinctly in his mind that he actually sees it in the wood before him...[4]

"His taste is refined, talent versatile, fancy sublime, and imagination inventive... the mere overflow of his mind would make a reputation for the common run of architects and artists."[5]

Descriptions of Hammatt Billings by his contemporaries

After advertising for architects, and nearly finalizing a deal in Pilgrim Hall, Hammatt Billings interrupted the process and presented a plan that was so attractive it was eventually approved in 1855. Billings' plan was to build two monuments (Forefathers', and a canopy over Plymouth Rock). In addition, he offered to organize and raise the funds himself! He offered steel-plate pictures and engravings as well as twenty-three inch high statuettes to contributors of $150 to $400.

Hammat Billings was born in Boston in 1818. At a young age he exhibited great talent in drawing and became an apprentice as a teenager. Billings was also very broad in his talent. In addition to doing sculpture, he designed buildings, illustrated books and painted pictures. What seemed providential at the time was that he was a scholar in both Biblical and historic themes. Billings once painted sixty murals on the book of Revelation (the last book of the Bible)! Thus, it is no wonder that his choice of symbols on the monument weave together in symbolism the Pilgrim story with their beliefs from the Bible.

CONSTRUCTION OF FOREFATHERS' MONUMENT

Construction of Forefathers' Monument
(used by permission-Pilgrim Society)

"...Out of their trials and sorrows we pluck prosperity and happiness; from their oppression springs our freedom... It is for this we bid the monumental shaft rise to Heaven. It is for this we are assembled by thousands to cheer on the work, and implore the blessing of Heaven upon its progress and its completion."[6] Remarks at the August 3, 1859 Celebration in Plymouth

Although the cornerstone was laid in 1859, and the Canopy over the Rock was finished in 1867, the construction of Forefathers' Monument seemed to go nowhere. By 1874, Hammatt Billings and the Pilgrim Society realized that because of the cost of the Civil War, the entire monument would have to be cut to half of its original size. Then, in November of that year,

Billings died. Joseph, his brother and partner, continued the work.

In 1875, the pedestal was completed, with the central figure of Faith put in place by 1877. Morality was set in 1878. However, in 1880, Joseph Billings died, and Rev. Harding, the financial agent of the project also passed away. Though this left the Pilgrim Society with the entire project, they, like the Pilgrims they commemorated, pressed on in spite of these obstacles, erecting a monument to the faith that was the cause of their perserverance.

The seated statue of Education was set in 1881, and in 1886 the seated figure of Liberty was put in place. It was not until 1888 that the final seated figure of Law was put in its place and the monument completed.

It was now time for a dedication ceremony that the town of Plymouth would not soon forget. The entire monument cost more than $150,000 and its funds came from more than 11,000 people. The Dedication Celebration took place in August 1, 1889. From the ringing of bells at 6 A.M. to the Ball at the Armory at 10 P.M., it was indeed a celebration of Plymouth's forefathers in grand style.

"In the name of the Fathers we dedicate this monument and ourselves. For ages it will stand the enduring witness to grave and resolute conduct; to privations and sacrifices; to thrift and frugality; to domestic love and unaffected piety; to rectitude in thought as well as in life; to earnest principles and true beliefs; to Christian fidelity and faith... here and now we rededicate ourselves to a more fervent love for man as man; to a braver allegiance to truth for truth's sake, and this 'in the name of God' and Amen and Amen!"[7] Remarks by William C.P. Breckinridge at the 1889 Dedication

DEDICATORY PLAQUE

Dedicatory Plaque

National Monument to the Forefathers, Erected by a Grateful People, In Remembrance of their labors, sacrifices and sufferings for the cause of civil and religious liberty

"Let us not forget the religious character of our origin. Our fathers were brought hither by their high veneration for the Christian religion. They journeyed by its light, and labored in its hope. They sought to incorporate its principles with the elements of their society, and to diffuse its influence through all their institutions, civil, political or literary..."[8] Remarks by Daniel Webster at the Dedication of Pilgrim Hall, 1820

The Pilgrims believed that religious liberty preceded civil liberty. The first was internal, the second external. Religious (or Christian) liberty gave rise to civil liberty in society. However, the civil liberty defined by the Pilgrims would be quite different than how it is defined today. Civil liberty today is based upon pluralism and religious neutrality whereas the Pilgrim would have desired a society singularly based upon Christianity as the source of its laws.

It is interesting to note that the Monument is best interpreted in the historical context of its time by beginning with Faith and moving to Morality, Law, Education and Liberty in that order. The internal religious liberty is best expressed by Faith and Morality, whereas the external liberty is best expressed by Law, Education and Liberty.

FAITH

Statue of Faith

"True it was that such attempts were not to be made and undertaken without good ground and reason, not rashly or lightly as many have done for curiosity or hope of gain, etc. But their condition was not ordinary, their ends were good and honorable, their calling lawful and urgent; and therefore they might expect the blessing of God in their proceeding. Yea, though they should lose their lives in this action, yet might they have comfort in the same and their endeavors would be honorable."[9]

There are four key symbols on this statue of Faith that Hammatt Billings uses to interpret the Pilgrim beliefs that would also be shared by all who experienced the historic reformation in the

1500s. In other words, these four characteristics define a forefather in general, and a pilgrim in particular (male or female).

The Open Bible—Faith is holding a Bible that is depicted as open, or its pages being blown by the wind. The Bible used by the Pilgrims and known as the "Book of the Reformation" was the Geneva Edition which was small enough to carry, cheap enough to own, and easy enough for the individual to study since it was divided into chapter and verses for the first time in history. The Pilgrims on the *Mayflower* brought the Geneva Edition, whereas those not joined with the Separatist movement owned the State-sanctioned Bible of their day, the King James Version. The Pilgrims believed that the Bible was infallible, and the only source and standard for their personal lives, as well as the governing of their families, churches and society.

Cropped enlargement of the Open Bible on Faith

"When as by the travail and diligence of some godly and zealous peachers, and God's blessing on their labors, as in other places of the land, so in the North parts, many became enlightened by the Word of God and had their ignorance and sins discovered unto them, and began by His grace to reform their lives."[10]

The Raised Forefinger – Billings depicts Faith pointing to Heaven. This is the Pilgrim belief that there is only one way to the Father and Heaven, and that is through Jesus Christ, His only begotten Son. A major tenet of faith that defined a reformer was the belief in the priesthood of all believers. In other words, there was only one mediator between God and man: Jesus Christ. There was no need to pray through a bishop or priest in order to get to God, for one could have a direct relationship with God through Christ. This truth defined the reformation, caused much controversy, and split the church into two factions. Bradford describes the contest with these words:

Cropped enlargement of the Raised forefinger

"The one side labored to have the right worship of God and discipline of Christ established in the church, according to the simplicity of the gospel, without the mixture of men's inventions, and to have and to be ruled by the laws of God's Word... The other party, though under many colors and pretences, endeavored to have the episcopal dignity (after the popish manner) with their large power and jurisdiction still retained... and enabled them with lordly and tyrannous power to persecute the poor servants of God."[11]

The Star on Faith's Forehead – A star represents honor and importance. The star on Faith's forehead can depict the high place that the intellect and mind had among reformers and Pilgrims alike. The mind was a gift from God, and though fallible due to sin, it could be guided by the revelation of God's Word, applying eternal truths to every practical situation faced by an individual in life. In other words, the Bible had answers to life's difficulties, but the application of Biblical truth had to be carefully reasoned from the Scriptures in a logical manner. This is why the Pilgrim as well as the Puritan (general term for reformers) placed such an importance upon education, books, and literacy. Bradford describes this truth by relating the ministry of their pastor in England and Holland, John Robinson, applying Biblical truth to secular issues.

Cropped enlargement of the star on her forehead

"For besides his singular abilities in divine things (wherein he excelled) he was also very able to give directions in civil affairs and to foresee dangers and inconveniences, by which means he was very helpful to their outward estates and so was every way as a common father unto them."[12]

100

Faith's Foot on Plymouth Rock—Faith is stepping forward, with her left foot on Plymouth Rock. Not only did Hammatt Billings design two monuments, he linked the Pilgrim faith in God to their arrival here on the shores of Plymouth in 1620. Faith is looking in an easterly direction, or the direction from which the Pilgrims sailed from England. A Pilgrim believed that all events in life are governed by the Providence of God. Internal faith in God will result in external obedience and when one looks back on past events, one can see the Hand of God—or Providence—directing those events.

Cropped enlargement of Faith's foot on the Rock

"Being thus constrained to leave their native soil and country, their lands and livings, and all their friends and familiar acquaintance, it was thought marvelous by many... But these things did not dismay them, though they did sometimes trouble them; for their desires were set on the ways of God and to enjoy His ordinances, but they rested on His providence, and knew Whom they had believed."[13]

The Pilgrim believed that the Bible, in its original languages, was the ultimate source and standard for their personal lives. They recognized Jesus Christ as the Son of God and the only mediator to a relationship with God the Father. They also believed the Bible had been opened by the Providential Hand of God so that they could reform their lives by actively reasoning from its principles and laws to their present situation. Finally, they embraced a providential view of history, and rested on the fact that God was directing their lives, ultimately bringing them from England to Plymouth Rock.

It is interesting to note that honorable William Ames, Governor of Plymouth, paid for this statue in order that it be placed on the pedestal. This monument has been fondly called "Faith" Monument for years in honor of the beliefs of the Pilgrims.

MORALITY

Morality

"It is well known unto the godly and judicious, how ever since the first breaking out of the light of the gospel in our honorable nation of England... what wars and oppositions ever since, Satan hath raised, maintained and continued against the Saints."[14]

Morality is the first seated figure, about 15 feet high, that explains the internal faith of the Pilgrims with greater clarity. She is looking heavenward from which she gains her source from God and the Bible. Morality encompasses the religious convictions that one holds regarding how a person is to live. The Pilgrim convictions in morality brought them into conflict with their age.

The Ten Commandments define one's relationship to God (first four) and man (last six). We have already noted the Pilgrims' desire to obey God's law as it related to their relationship with Him. However, it is of note that Bradford describes their obedience to the last six by indicating how the Dutch reacted to their godly character:

103

Cropped enlargement of Ten Commandments of Morality

"Though many of them were poor, yet there was none so poor that if they were known to be of that congregation the Dutch (either bakers or others) would trust them in any reasonable matter when they wanted money, because they had found by experience how careful they were to keep their

word, and saw them so painful and diligent in their callings. Yea, they would strive to get their custom and to employ them above others in their work, for their honesty and diligence."[15]

The scroll of Revelation is the last book of the Bible and it describes the rise of antichristian behavior and the rule of ungodliness in a culture. Though written as a warning to the first century believers, the Pilgrims, as did many of their time, interpreted this symbolic book as applying in principle to the day in which they lived. Hammatt Billings was familiar with this book, having painted 60 murals on its contents, and it was also the first book of the Bible translated into common English by John Wycliffe in the late 1300s to help believers understand the corruption that had come in both church and state.

Cropped enlargement of scroll of Revelation

"And this contention died not with Queen Mary, nor was left beyond the seas. But at her death these people returning into England under gracious Queen Elizabeth, many of them being preferred to bishoprics and other promotions according to their aims and desires, that inveterate hatred against the holy discipline of Christ in His church hath continued to this day."[165]

The collar of Morality, similar to the breastplate worn by the High Priest, symbolizes the fact that each Pilgrim was a priest before God, taking the state of their nation to God in prayer as well as action. The Pilgrims were called Separatists because they separated from the established church, and formed their own churches by a voluntary covenant. The church covenant was established at Scrooby in 1606.

105

Cropped enlargement of collar of Morality

"So many, therefore, of these professors as saw th evil of these things in these parts, and whose hearts the Lord had touched with heavenly zeal for His truth, they shook off this yoke of antichristian bondage, and as the Lord's free people joined themselves (by a covenant of the Lord) into a church estate, in the fellowship of the gospel, to walk in all His ways made known, or to be made known unto them, according to their best endeavors, whatsoever it should cost them, the Lord assisting them."[17]

The statuette of the prophet under the left side of Morality's chair depicts the fact that the Pilgrims heard a call from God to leave England and go to Holland where they thought there would be religious liberty. Note the prophet is looking heavenward receiving a call from God.

THE PROPHET

The Prophet

"Yet these and many other sharper things which afterward befell them, were no other than they looked for, and therefore were better prepared to bear them by the assistance of God's grace and Spirit. Yet seeing themselves thus molested, and that there was no hope of their continuance there, by a joint consent they resolved to go into the Low Countries, where they heard there was freedom of religion for all men."

The statuette of the evangelist under the right side of Morality's chair depicts the fact that the Pilgrims had a desire to be the foundation of a better society by first exercising their religion and morality, and attempting to be an example to the native Indians as well as others who would come later on. Note that the evangelist is taking seed from the Bible and throwing on the ground, a common symbol for preaching the gospel.

THE EVANGELIST

The Evangelist

"Lastly (and which was not least), a great hope and inward zeal they had of laying some good foundation or at least to make some way thereunto, for the propagating and advancing the gospel of the kingdom of Christ in those remote parts of the world; yea, though they should be but even as stepping-stones unto others for the performing of so great a work."[18]

The Pilgrims attempted to leave England in 1607, but were betrayed and several of the leaders spent time in prison. Then in 1608, after a near ship-wreck, they made it to Holland. After spending one year in Amsterdam, and eleven in Leyden, where they grew to a congregation of nearly three hundred, they left Holland for the new world. Though many reasons contributed to this move, Bradford describes their leaving in this manner:

ALTO-RELIEF OF THE EMBARKATION

Alto-Relief

"So they left that goodly and pleasant city (Delftshaven), which had been their resting place near twelve years; but they knew they were pilgrims, and looked not much on those things, but lift up their eyes to the heavens, their dearest country, and quieted their spirits."[19]

Morality was paid for by the State Legislature of Massachusetts. It was thought that the legislature and its public servants ought to be a clear example of morality, demonstrating leadership for the citizens. In like manner, the State Legislature of Connecticut paid for the alto-relief of the Embarkation, since it was a Puritan remnant embracing Pilgrim ideas of government led by Thomas Hooker that embarked to Connecticut, founding Hartford, Whethersfield and Windsor.

109

LIST OF MAYFLOWER PASSENGERS

Mayflower *Passenger List*

"The names of those which came over first, in the year 1620, and were by the blessing of God the first beginners and in a sort the foundation of all the Plantations and Colonies in New England; and their families. "[20] William Bradford explaining his list of passengers

This list of passengers is part two from the other side of the monument. Note some of the names of the Pilgrim children. About one quarter of the way up, William White's sons are Resolved and Peregrine. Pilgrims often named their children using character qualities (such as Resolved) much like names were given in the Old Testament of the Bible. It was not unusual to have names like Faith, Hope, Humility and Charity. There are several historic societies which exist for the purpose of preserving the identity of *Mayflower* descendents.

LAW

Law

"For God being the God of Order, and not of confusion, hath commanded in His Word, and put man into a capacity in some measure to observe and be guided by good and wholesome laws; which are so far good and wholesome, as by how much they are derived from, and agreeable to the ancient platform of God's Law." [21] Preamble to the 1671 Edition of Pilgrim Laws

The statue of Law has powerful eyes that pierce right through the observer, convicting him of wrong-doing. The art of the 1800s, during the Victorian era, depicted heart-felt beliefs and home duties as female, and leadership and defensive responsibilities as male. Thus, Law is depicted as male.

111

One hand is extended toward the victim in mercy, while the other holds the statute laws of society. The Pilgrim believed that all were equal before the law, and no special privileges should be given due to birth, wealth or social status. Many of their laws came right from the Bible, and others applied Biblical principles to justice, ethics and proper restitution for wrongs done.

Cropped enlargement of statute book and outstretched hand

Historian Robert Bartlett notes that the Pilgrim exercised more tolerance toward those that differed with them than many of the puritan sects that settled in Boston. However, in order to live with the Pilgrims and enjoy the liberty and justice they practiced, one had to agree to have the Bible be the base of the legal system. Thus, religious liberty was under the law of God, not a system of neutrality or the existence of a secular state.[22]

JUSTICE

Justice

"This year John Billington the elder, one that came over with the first, was arraigned, and both by grand and petty jury found guilty of willful murder, by plain and notorious evidence. And was for the same accordingly executed. This, as it was the first execution amongst them, so was it a matter of great sadness unto them."[23] Bradford's comments in the year 1630

"Yet some of the rude and ignorant sort murmured that any English should be put to death for the Indians... And so, upon the forementioned evidence, were cast by the jury and condemned, and executed for the same, September 4. And some of the Narragansett Indians and of the party's friends were present when it was done, which gave them and all the country good satisfaction."[24] Bradford relating the execution of three white men for the murder of a Narragansett Indian in the year 1638

Though stern justice was enacted by practicing due process of law as the Bible describes (with two or three witnesses required before the death penalty could be utilized), it was also done with equity. The depiction of scales of justice indicates the practice of law and equity that had been inherited from the common law of England. The combination of law and equity in the same court insured that the punishment would fit the crime and was an improvement on the separate courts of law and equity in England guilt that could result in a punishment that was far more severe than the crime.

MERCY

Mercy

"But by the former passages, and other things of like nature, they began to see that Squanto sought his own ends and played his own game, by putting the Indians in fear and drawing gifts from them to enrich himself, making them believe he could stir up war against whom he would, and make peace for whom he would."[25]

Squanto was called by Bradford "a gift from God" due to his ability to translate between the two cultures. However, Squanto was also a character that caused mischief and on several occasions told the Pilgrims that Massasoit was going to attack, and then when it didn't happen, he took the credit for stopping it. When Massasoit asked for Squanto's death, Bradford desired mercy, thinking that this punishment did not fit the crime, and they also needed Squanto to continue proper relations with the Indians. It was the practice of lawful justice that allowed the Pilgrim to share their faith and it be received the Natives.

ALTO-RELIEF OF THE PEACE TREATY

Peace Treaty Alto-Relief

"...Their great sagamore Massasoit was hard by, with Quadequina his brother, and all their men. Our messenger made a speech unto him that King James saluted him with words of love and peace, and did accept of him as his friend and ally, and that our governor desired to see him and to truck with him, and to confirm peace with him, as his next neighbor." [26] The Peace Treaty enacted between Massasoit of the Wompanoags and John Carver, Governor of the Pilgrim Colony

"1. That neither he nor any of his should injure or do hurt to any of our people. 2. And if any of his did hurt to any of ours, he should send the offender, that we might punish him. 3. That if any of our tools were taken away, when our people were at work, he should cause them to be restored; and if ours did any harm to any of his, we would do the like to them. 4. If any did unjustly war against him, we would aid him; if any did war against us, he should aid us. 5. He should send to his neighbor confederates to certify them of this, that they might not wrong us, but might be likewise comprised in the conditions of peace. 6. That when their men came to us, they should leave their bows and arrows behind them, as we should do our pieces when we came to them."[27]

116

By allowing each culture or nation to punish offenders according to their own law, and to negotiate without weapons, it began a trust between the Pilgrims and their nearest neighbors that lasted more than 50 years!

This statue of Law was put in place primarily by a grant from a group of Connecticut lawyers. The link between the Pilgrim ideas of law and government and the founding of Connecticut (the Constitution state) cannot be minimized. Connecticut's Fundamental Orders of 1639 constructs a bicameral legislature. Noah Webster's *Sketches of American Policy*, suggesting that the United States Constitution be similar to that of Connecticut, was put before George Washington prior to the Constitutional Convention. It was Roger Sherman from Connecticut that broke deadlock at the Convention to adopt a bicameral legislature in our national constitution.

ONE SMALL CANDLE QUOTE

One Small Candle Quote

"Thus out of small beginnings greater things have been produced by His hand that made all things from nothing, and gives being to all things that are; and, as one small candle may light a thousand, so the light here kindled hath shone unto many, yea in some sort to our whole nation; let the glorious name of Jehovah have all the praise."[28] William Bradford's comments on the year 1630

The West Panel and its quote from William Bradford is the newest edition to the monument, having been placed through the generous gift of Verna Orndorff in preparation for the centennial celebration in 1989. Just as Faith faces the harbor from where the Pilgrims came, so this quote faces Westward in the direction of the expanding nation that grew from the Pilgrim ideal. It was Faith that brought the Pilgrim to Plymouth Rock, and it was their "small beginning" that eventually reached "our whole nation."

Many of the ideas and beliefs of the Pilgrims in respect to government (representation), economics (free enterprise), liberty (God-given rights protected by government), private property (the public recording or registry of deeds so that a missing deed wouldn't result in the loss of ownership), marriage and the home as the cornerstone of society (marriage was a civil ceremony and not just religious) and freedom of religious expression all flowered into the American culture many years later. Bradford wrote this phrase at the close of his commentary on the year 1630 describing the Pilgrim church government of electing elders and not requiring one to be a member of the church in order to vote in civil affairs having an impact upon the puritans. However, it was the seed or beginning of a greater impact in general.

Education

"... they saw that their posterity would be in danger to degenerate and be corrupted."[29]

Education is the most youthful of all the seated statues. She is female, indicating one of the major concerns and duties of the women would be the instruction of their children in the home. Indeed, it was a concern for their children and future generations that was one of the reasons why the Pilgrim risked coming to the new world.

She is wearing a wreath of learning on her head, indicating the high expectations placed upon youth by the Pilgrims. Female children were expected to learn to cook, sew and do household duties by the age of five or six. Male children worked with their fathers in the fields at an early age as well. Strict discipline was enforced by parents, with attitudes being corrected long before bad habits and behavior would be displayed. It

119

was this high expectation, but the unfortunate weight of responsibility, that caused the Pilgrims to consider coming to the new world.

Cropped enlargement of wreath

120

"For many of their children that were of best dispositions and gracious inclinations, having learned to bear the yoke in their youth and willing to bear part of their parents' burden, were oftentimes so oppressed with their heavy labors that though their minds were free and willing, yet their bodies bowed under the weight of the same, and became decrepit in their youth..."[30]

Education is pointing to a book of knowledge. The book of knowledge could be the Bible, but the Pilgrims were also quite literate in many other works as well. The teaching of children to read at an early age at home, coupled with the fact that literacy was very high among those who held to the teachings of the Reformation, make this symbol on the monument historically accurate. Though the Pilgrims did not start a grammar school in the early years, their literacy was high due to the home education practiced.

Cropped enlargement of book of knowledge

121

"4ᵗʰ Objection; Children not catechized nor taught to read. Answer: Neither is true, for diverse take pains with their own as they can. Indeed, we have no common school for want of a fit person, or hitherto means to maintain one; though we desire now to begin."³¹ Bradford answering an accusation made in 1624 that a lack of a school suggested that children were not being taught to read

Bradford's Bible
(used by permission-Pilgrim Society)

"The number of volumes possessed by settlers in the colony was remarkable, considering the size of the community, the high price of books, and the scarcity of personally owned books in this era. Although admittedly some of these were heavy theology and beyond the grasp of the average colonist, their presence nevertheless indicated a veneration of learning and the fact that their religion was related to the best Protestant thought of the day. The general distribution of the Bible and the Ainsworth psalter proves that the majority did read and had a vital interest in their religion."[32] Historian Robert Bartlett on the literacy of the Pilgrims

Almost everyone owned a Bible, and a few of the Pilgrim leaders (Brewster, Bradford and Winslow) owned between 300 and 400 volumes. Myles Standish and Edward Winslow learned the Indian dialect. William Bradford had a hobby of studying Hebrew by candlelight in the wilderness. His Hebrew Exercises are an example of the scholarship and intellectual literacy among Pilgrim leaders.

YOUTH

Youth

"Of all sorrows most heavy to be borne, was that many of their children, by these occasions and the great licentiousness of youth in the country, and the manifold temptations of the place, were drawn away by evil examples into extravagant and dangerous courses, getting the reins off their necks and departing from their parents."[33]
Bradford describing life in Holland

The statuette underneath the left side of Education depicts the fact that the Pilgrims had a concern for their children and the fact that they were being led astray by bad examples. Here a mother leads her child, taking responsibility to do what is necessary to preserve both the innocence as well as the purity of child training.

123

Wisdom

"...they saw and found by experience the hardness of the place and country to be such as few in comparison would come to them... they saw that though the people generally bore all these difficulties very cheerfully and with a resolute courage, being in the best and strength of their years, yet old age began to steal on many of them. "[34] Bradford describing two other reasons for leaving Holland

The wisdom of experience and age is depicted here as the means of leading youth. Once leaving England and their agricultural lifestyle, and then learning new trades in Holland (such as weaving and cloth), the experience had in this caused them to wonder if time began to work against them. They wanted to practice their faith freely and let it produce a society built upon Biblical premises. When would they have a chance to do that if they remained? Wisdom dictated making the move at that time.

ALTO-RELIEF OF THE SIGNING OF THE MAYFLOWER COMPACT

Signing of Mayflower *Compact*

"Occasioned partly by the discontented and mutinous speeches that some of the strangers amongst them and let fall from them in the ship; that when they came ashore they would use their own liberty, for none had power to command them, the patent they had being for Virginia and not for New England... and partly that such an act by them done, this their condition considered, might be as firm as any patent, and in some respects more sure."[35] Bradford's description as to why the Compact was written

The Mayflower Compact of 1620, written on board the *Mayflower* in Provincetown harbor, is the precursor of the practice of self-government and constitutional law in New England in particular and the United States in general. Having been blown off course, and out of the jurisdiction of their original patent for northern Virginia, they wrote their own document to bring unity and remove dissension.

In essence, it was an extension of their church covenant formed in Scrooby in 1606. The model of voluntary association through covenant accountability in the church now became a reality within the civil structure of the budding community. The jurisdictional distinction between church and state was the seed of what was to come in America. This would mark the development of American government from its theological roots within the historic Reformation of Europe.

THE MAYFLOWER COMPACT OF 1620

"In the Name of God, Amen. We whose names are underwritten, the loyal subjects of our dread Sovereign Lord King James, by the Grace of God of Great Britain, France, and Ireland King, Defender of the Faith, etc. Having undertaken for the Glory of God and advancement of the

Christian Faith and Honor of our King and Country, a Voyage to plant the First Colony in the Northern Parts of Virginia, do by these presents solemnly and mutually in the presence of God and one of another, Covenant and Combine ourselves together into a Civil Body Politic, for our better ordering and preservation and furtherance of the ends aforesaid, and by virtue hereof to enact, constitute and frame such just and equal Laws, Ordinances, Acts, Constitutions and Offices, from time to time, as shall be thought most meet and convenient for the general good of the Colony, unto which we promise all due submission and obedience. In witness whereof we have herunto subscribed our names at Cape Cod, the 11th of November, in the year of the reign of our Sovereign Lord King James, of England, France and Ireland the eighteenth, and of Scotland the fifty-fourth. Anno Domini 1620."[36]

Note that the order of giving allegiance and glory to God and then one's Country became the order for most preambles and documents of law written in the colonies up through and including the Declaration of Independence in 1776. The pattern is consistent with the Reformation thinking of the time for both Pilgrim and Puritan.

Most males probably signed the Compact. It is presumed that those that did not sign it were too sick to put their signature to the document. The original has been lost, but one year later England issued the Pierce Patent to make the Pilgrim settlement legal from their perspective. It treated Bradford as proprietor, potentially putting all land and power in his hands. Thus, though the Pilgrim governed himself by the Mayflower Compact, (Bradford giving the power back to the people under their civil covenant), from England's point of view, their real government document was the Pierce Patent of 1621. The original of this document is on display in Pilgrim Hall Museum.

MAYFLOWER PASSENGER LIST

Mayflower Passenger List

"I cannot but here take occasion not only to mention but greatly to admire the marvelous providence of God! That notwithstanding the many changes and hardships that these people went through, and the many enemies they had and difficulties they met withal, that so many of them should live to very old age!"[37] Bradford describing in the year 1643 the fact that many Pilgrims lived to 60, 65, or 70 when the average life span was 40!

This list, which is actually part one found in the original *Of Plymouth Plantation*, lists some of the leaders and their children. Note that the first three individuals listed, John Carver (who died the first winter), William Bradford (died at age 67 in 1657) and Edward Winslow were the first three governors of the Colony. William Brewster (who died in 1643 at the age of 83) was the Elder of the church, since their Pastor, John Robinson, did not come to Plymouth, and died in Holland in 1625.

Note the sons of William Brewster, Love and Wrestling. Brewster remarked that he named his son Love so that he might "love God with all his heart" and his other son Wrestling that he might "wrestle with the devil" all his life as well. Brewster may have named his children in order to fulfill the destiny for which he felt they were called.

LIBERTY

Liberty

"Whereas you are become a body politic, using amongst yourselves civil government, and are not furnished with any persons of special eminency above the rest, to be chosen by you into office of government, let your wisdom and godliness appear, not only choosing such persons as do entirely love and will promote the common good, but also in yielding unto them all due honor and obedience in their lawful administrations, not beholding in them the ordinariness of their persons, but God's ordinance for your good..."[38]

Pastor John Robinson in his farewell letter in 1620

The advice of their pastor, John Robinson, to first deal with their relationship to God and then one another (religious liberty), also led to sound counsel in relation to civil affairs (civil liberty) when he stated what is written above in his farewell letter of 1620. The symbolism on this seated statue exceeds the others as it depicts the progression of liberty from the internal (religious) to the external (civil).

Note the slain lion on the back of Liberty. A lion symbolized both Satan from a theological point of view and tyranny from an historic point of view. It was the faith and practice of the Christian religion of the Pilgrims that defeated the lion of spiritual and natural oppression. Bradford opens his journal *Of Plymouth Plantation* with these analogies.

Liberty and Slain Lion

131

"What wars and oppositions ever since, Satan hath raised, maintained and continued against the Saints, from time to time, in one sort or other. Sometimes by bloody death and cruel torments, other whiles imprisonments, banishments and other hard usages; as being loath his kingdom should go down, the truth prevail and the churches of God revert to their ancient purity and recover their primitive order, liberty and beauty....

With all those courts, canons and ceremonies, together with all such livings, revenues and subordinate officers, with other such means as formerly upheld their antichristian greatness and enabled them with lordly and tyrannous power to persecute the poor servants of God."[39]

The broken chains about the ankles and wrists depict liberty from the chains of oppression, both spiritual (religious) as well as natural (civil). Their freedom is first depicted by Bradford as spiritual. However, as the Mayflower Compact states, the purpose of civil government is to protect God-given liberty and equal rights common to all:

Cropped enlargement of broken chains

"Covenant and Combine ourselves together into a Civil Body Politic, for our better ordering and preservation and furtherance of the ends aforesaid, and by virtue hereof to enact, constitute and frame such just and equal Laws, Ordinances, Acts, Constitutions and Offices, from time to time, as shall be thought most meet and convenient for the general good of the Colony, unto which we promise all due submission and obedience."

From the Mayflower Compact

This is the strongest of all the statues. The armor is in the Roman style, and depicts the defense of one's spiritual (or religious) liberty; as well as natural (or civil) liberty. The Book of Ephesians in the Bible describes one's spiritual defenses in the analogy of Roman armor, and this may have been where Hammatt Billings got this symbolism. The spiritual armor of faith, patience and fortitude is described by Bradford:

Cropped enlargement of breastplate and armor

"Being now come into the Low Countries (Holland)... it was not long before they saw the grim and grisly face of poverty coming upon them like an armed man, with whom they must buckle and encounter, and from whom they could not fly. But they were armed with faith and patience against him and all his encounters."[40] Bradford describing the challenges of new life in Holland

Liberty's sword is sheathed in a defensive position as well. The Pilgrims believed they ought to defend themselves, but not aggressively begin a war that was unnecessary. A fort and pallisade walls were completed in 1622-23 for the purpose of self-defense.

134

Cropped enlargement of sword

"This summer they built a fort with good timber, both strong and comely, which was of good defense, made with flat roof and battlements, on which their ordinance were mounted, where they

kept constant watch, especially in time of danger. It served them also for a meeting house."[41]
Bradford describing the Pilgrim defense against external Danger

OVERTHROW OF TYRANNY

Tyranny

"It was answered, that all great and honorable actions were accompanied with great difficulties, and must be both enterprised and overcome with answerable courages. It was granted the dangers were great, but not desperate. The difficulties were great, but not invincible."[42]

"It might be sundry of the things feared might never befall; others by provident care and the use of good means might in a great measure be prevented; and all of them, through the help of God, by fortitude and patience, might either be borne or overcome."[43] Bradford describing the dangers of the New World

The Pilgrim relied upon their character to overthrow the tyrannical oppression in church or state. Here they depict the overthrow of fear that faced them as they were deciding whether they would come to the new world. Whether in church or state, or in facing internal or external danger, the Pilgrim thought that overcoming these would come from within, a defense of attitude, character and fortitude. The Pilgrim had faced in England the tyranny of both church and state as well:

"The work of God was no sooner manifest in them but presently they were both scoffed and scorned by the profane multitude; and the ministers urged with subscription, or else must be silenced. And the poor people were so vexed with apparitors and pursuivants and the commisary courts, as truly their affliction was not small."[44] Bradford relating the ecclesiastical and civil tyranny in England

136

PEACE

Peace

"Which, notwithstanding, they bore sundry years with much patience, till they were occasioned by the continuance and increase of these troubles, and other means which the Lord raised up in those days, to see further into things by the light of the Word of God. How not only these base and beggerly ceremonies were unlawful, but also that the lordly and tyrannous power of the prelates ought not to be submitted unto; which thus, contrary to the freedom of the gospel, would load and burden men's consciences and by their compulsory power make a profane mixture of persons and things in the worship of God."[45]

Bradford describing the Pilgrim peaceful resistance to Tyranny

137

The Pilgrims' peaceful resistance to tyranny caused them to ultimately separate from the Church of England, and for a time worship illegally and underground. It was their resistance in religious matters that gave them the conviction to be willing to suffer loss or even death for their convictions. Regardless of whether we believe everything these Pilgrim forefathers believed, we must respect their conviction to abide by these peacefully, and through time, overthrow tyranny in both church and state.

ALTO-RELIEF OF THE LANDING OF THE PILGRIMS

Landing of the Pilgrims

"What could now sustain them but the Spirit of God and His grace? May not and ought not the children of these fathers rightly say: 'Our fathers were Englishmen which came over this great ocean, and were ready to perish in this wilderness, but they cried unto the Lord, and He head their voice and looked on their adversity', etc. 'Let them therefore praise the Lord, because He is good, and His mercies endure forever.' 'Yea, let them which have been redeemed of the Lord, show how He hath delivered them from the hand of the oppressor. When they wandered in the desert wilderness out of the way, and found no city to dwell in, both hungry and thirsty, their soul was overwhelmed in them. Let them confess before the Lord His lovingkindness and His wonderful works before the sons of men."

Bradford's reaction to the landing of the Pilgrims in the New World

The Pilgrims landed in Plymouth on Monday, December 11, 1620, after thirty days of exploration on Cape Cod looking for a suitable place to build the first Common House. Only men were in the shallop, for the Mayflower was still anchored in Provincetown harbor. This magnificent monument begins with the faith of the Pilgrims in England, and concludes with their landing on Plymouth Rock.

"... let us remember the solemn admonition of him who brought gifts to the altar and remember that if thy brother has aught against thee, 'leave then thy gift upon the altar and go to thy brother.' If we, the descendants of the Pilgrims, have been wanting in their stern energy, in their unflinching intrepidity against wrong – if we have been proud and cruel – if against the poor and oppressed of our country we have closed our affections, these our brethren have much against us."[46]

Remarks at the August 3, 1859 Celebration in Plymouth

May these truths and lessons inspire you to emulate the positive attributes of our forefathers to affect generations to come! May we have the gratitude, faith in God, fortitude and patience of our forefathers as we face the dangers, opportunities and challenges of the 21st century!

ABOUT THE AUTHOR

Dr. Paul Jehle has worked as a volunteer tour guide in the town of Plymouth since 1978. An active member of the Pilgrim Society and Old Colony Club, he served on the Education Committee of the Centennial Celebration of Forefathers' Monument in 1989 and the 375th Town Celebration of the Pilgrim Landing in 1995. He has also served as the Education Director of Plymouth Rock Foundation since 1988. Dr. Jehle is an author, historian and lecturer on the Pilgrims. He is Senior Pastor of The New Testament Church in Cedarville (south Plymouth), and Principal of The New Testament Christian School, where young people in junior-senior high school, as part of their curriculum, train as volunteer guides for the Pilgrim Monuments.

ABOUT PLYMOUTH ROCK FOUNDATION

Chartered by John G. Talcott, Jr. and Charles H. Wolfe in 1971, the Plymouth Rock Foundation has as its mission the preservation of materials and primary source documents on the Pilgrims and America's historic and religious heritage. In addition to publishing books and materials, it holds an annual conference on America's history as well as sponsoring the *America's Hometown Thanksgiving Celebration* that takes place the weekend prior to Thanksgiving.

ABOUT VISION FORUM

Vision Forum Ministries is a 501(c)(3) organization based in San Antonio, Texas, which sponsors conferences for fathers and sons, trains leaders to better understand America's rich legal tradition, and produces information designed to encourage family and cultivate an appreciation for America's great Christian heritage. Each year, Vision Forum Ministries sponsors a Faith and Freedom Tour in locations like New England and Virginia. For more information, visit www.visionforum.org

INDEX TO ILLUSTRATIONS OF SUBJECTS & LOCATIONS

PART ONE

Plymouth Tour Map
between Part One and Part Two

PART TWO

ENDNOTES

[1] Everett, Edward, *Oration Delivered in Plymouth*, 1824, Pilgrim Hall Archives, page 61.

[2] *The Constitutional Articles of the Pilgrim Society*, printed by Allen Danforth, 1823, preamble, page 1.

[3] *An Account of the Pilgrim Celebration at Plymouth, August 1, 1853,* page 169, as reported by <u>The New York Mirror</u> Newspaper.

[4] Stoddard, Richard, *Hammatt Billings, Artist and Architect*, Old-Time New England, January-March, 1972, Vol. 62, No. 3, page 62.

[5] Jarves, James Jackson, writing in *The Art Idea,* 1864, *Ibid.,* page 76.

[6] Governor Banks of Massachusetts, *The Plymouth Rock*, August 4, 1859 edition.

[7] Breckinridge, William C.P., *An Account of the Pilgrim Celebration at Plymouth August 1, 1889.*, Pilgrim Hall Archives, page 106.

[8] Webster, Daniel, *Discourse Delivered at Plymouth, December 22, 1820,* Wells and Lilly, 1825, page 73; Pilgrim Hall Archives.

[9] Morison, Samuel Eliot, ed., *Of Plimoth Plantation*, by William Bradford, Alfred A. Knopf, 1979, page 27.

[10] *Ibid.,* page 8.

[11] *Ibid.,* page 6.

[12] *Ibid.,* page 18.

[13] *Ibid.,* page 11.

[14] *Ibid.,* page 3.

[15] *Ibid.,* page 20.

[16] *Ibid.,* page 6.

[17] *Ibid.,* page 9.

[18] *Ibid,* page 25.

[19] *Ibid.,* page 47.

[20] *Ibid.,* page 441.

[21] The Laws of the Pilgrims, a Facsimile Edition, Michael Glazier, Inc., and Pilgrim Society, 1977. The initial laws of the Pilgrims were compiled in 1636.

[22] Bartlett, Robert., Faith of the Pilgrims, United Church Press, 1978, chapter four "Outreach Toward Tolerance."

[23] *Of Plimoth Plantation,* Morison edition, page 234.

[24] *Ibid.,* pages 300-301.

[25] *Ibid.,* page 99.

[26] Fiore, Jordan, ed., Mourt's Relation, A Journal of the Pilgrims at Plymouth, first published in 1622, this edition published by the Plymouth Rock Foundation, 1985, page 49.

[27] *Ibid.,* page 49-50.

[28] *Of Plimoth Plantation,* Morison edition, page 236.

[29] *Ibid.,* page 25.

[30] *Ibid.,* page 24.

[31] *Ibid.,* page 143.

[32] Bartlett, Faith of the Pilgrims, page 44.

[33] *Of Plimoth Plantation,* Morison edition, page 25.

[34] *Ibid.,* pages 23, 24.

[35] *Ibid.,* page 75.

[36] *Ibid.,* pages 75-76.

[37] *Ibid.,* page 328.

[38] *Ibid.,* page 370.

[39] *Ibid.,* pages 1, 6.

[40] Morison, Samuel Eliot, ed., *Of Plimoth Plantation*, by William Bradford, Alfred A. Knopf, 1979, page 27.

[41] *Ibid.,* page 111.

[42] *Ibid.,* page 27.

[43] *Ibid.,* page 27.

[44] *Ibid.,* page 8.

[45] *Ibid.,* page 8.

[46] William Evarts of the New England Society, *The Plymouth Rock*, August 4, 1859 edition.

[47] Morison, Samuel Eliot, ed., *Of Plimoth Plantation*, by William Bradford, Alfred A. Knopf, 1979, pages 59-60.

[48] *Ibid.,* page 47.

[49] *Ibid.,* page 53.

[50] *Ibid.,* page 58.

[51] *Ibid.,* page 58.

[52] *Ibid.,* pages 58-59.

[53] *Ibid.,* page 59.

[54] *Ibid.,* pages 75-76.

[55] *Ibid.,* page 72.

[56] *Ibid.,* page 61.

[57] Fiore, Jordan, ed., *Mourt's Relation, A Journal of the Pilgrims at Plymouth.,* first published in 1622, republished by the Plymouth Rock Foundation, 1985, page 22.

[58] *Of Plimoth Plantation*, Morison edition, page 66.

[59] *Mourt's Relation*, pages 31-32.

[60] *Ibid.,* pages 32-33.

[61] *Ibid.,* page 33.

[62] Russell, Wm. S., *Pilgrim Memorials, and Guide to Plymouth*, Boston: Crosby and Nichols, 1864, page 23.

[63] Bittinger, Frederick W., *The Story of the Pilgrim Tercentenary Celebration at Plymouth in the Year 1921*, The Memorial Press, 1923, page 11.

[64] *Of Plimoth Plantation*, Morison edition, page 48.

[65] *Ibid.,* pages 11, 27.

[66] *Ibid.,* page 368.

[67] *Ibid.,* page 77.

[68] John 15:13.

[69] *Of Plimoth Plantation*, Morison edition, page 78.

[70] *Mourt's Relation*, page 50.

[71] *Of Plimoth Plantation*, Morison edition, page 79-80.

[72] *Ibid.,* page 81.

[73] *Mourt's Relation*, pages 48-50.

[74] *Ibid.,* page 60.

[75] *Ibid.,* page 71.

[76] Winslow, Edward., *Good Newes from New England*, first published in 1624, republished by Applewood Books, page 35.

[77] *Ibid.,* page 37.

[78] *Story of the Pilgrim Tercentenary*, page 119.

[79] *Ibid.,* page 120.

[80] Morton, *New England's Memorials*, Boston: Congregational Board, 1855, Pilgrim Hall Archives, pages 171-172.

[81] Mather, Cotton., *The Life of William Bradford*, from his *Magnalia*, 1852 edition, Pilgrim Hall Archives.

[82] Hoar, George, address in the 1901 edition.

[83] Hoar, George., address in the 1901 edition.

[84] Morison edition, page xxxv of the Introduction.

[85] *Mourt's Relation*, page 37.

[86] Morison edition, pages 325-327.

[87] *Mourt's Relation,* pages 38-39.

[88] *Of Plimoth Plantation*, Morison Edition, page 72.

[89] *Ibid.,* page 44.

[90] *Mourt's Relation*, page 49.

[91] *Of Plimoth Plantation*, Morison Edition, pages 223-224.

[92] *Mourt's Relation*, page 37.

[93] James, Sydney V., editor, *Three Visitors to Early Plymouth*, Plimoth Plantation, 1963, pages 75-76.

[94] Morison edition, page 111.

[95] Winslow, *Good Newes*, page 18.

[96] *Three Visitors*, pages 76-77.

[97] *Ibid.,* page 77.

[98] *Story of the Pilgrim Tercentenary*, page 28.

[99] Mather, Cotton, *Magnalia Christi Americana*, 1852 edition as reprinted in <u>The Hand of God in the Return of the Bradford Manuscript</u>, edited by Rosalie Slater and Verna Hall, Foundation for American Christian Education, 1971, pages 148-149.

FINI